To my daughter, Sophie,
who did not grow up in Africa
but may, one day,
understand my obsession with it

African Kingdoms of the Past

Zenj Buganda

•

East Africa

Kenny Mann

Dillon Press • Parsippany, New Jersey

ACKNOWLEDGMENTS

The author wishes to acknowledge the interest, patience, and expertise of the following consultants: Clarence G. Seckel, Jr., Curriculum Coordinator of Social Studies, School District 189. East Saint Louis, IL; Edna J. Whitfield, Social Studies Supervisor (retired), Saint Louis Public Schools, St. Louis, MO.

CREDITS

Design and Illustration: MaryAnn Zanconato
Picture Research: Kenny Mann and Valerie Vogel

PHOTO CREDITS

All photos by Silver Burdett Ginn unless otherwise noted.
Cover: Angela Fisher/Robert Estall Photo Agency. Courtesy, Department Library Services, American Museum of Natural History/Carl E. Akeley: 63. The American Numismatic Society: 22. Art Resource, NY/Werner Forman Archive: 41. The British Institute in Eastern Africa: 23. Copyright, British Museum: 70, 76. Cambridge University, Museum of Archaeology and Anthropology: 71. Camerapix: 15, 21, 96–97. Bruce Coleman, Inc./J.C. Carton: 54; R.A. Mittemeier: 10. Bernt Eichhorn: title page, 26–27, 31, 40, 92. Robert Estall Photo Agency/Angela Fisher: 37; Angela Fisher & Carol Beckwith: 8, 42–43. E. T. Archive: 50. Mary Evans Picture Library: 45, 59, 62. The Granger Collection, New York: 11. Hulton Deutsch Collection Limited: 64. The Hutchison Library: 38–39; T. Beddon: 48; Dave Brinicombe: 80–81. The Mansell Collection: 68. © National Geographic Society Image Collection/Gilberth Grosvenor: 66–67, 73. Peter Newark's Historical Pictures: 84. Popperfoto: 95. Superstock: 94. Maps: Ortelius Design: 6, 13, 61, 83.

Library of Congress Cataloging-in-Publication Data

Mann, Kenny.
    Zenj, Buganda : East Africa / Kenny Mann.—1st ed.
    p. cm.—African kingdoms of the past
    Includes bibliographical references and index.
    ISBN 0-87518-660-2 (JLSB).—ISBN 0-382-39658-8 (pbk.)
    1. Africa, East—History—To 1886—Juvenile literature. 2. Zanzibar—History—To 1890—Juvenile literature.
3. Uganda—History—To 1890—Juvenile literature. [1. Africa, East—History—To 1886.] I. Title. II. Series.
DT431.M25   1997   96-10618
967.6—dc20

Summary: This study of the ancient land of Zenj, which once occupied the coast, and the kingdom of Buganda, in the interior of East Africa, focuses on the legends, history, and lifeways of both indigenous peoples and immigrants and examines how trade and European colonization affected life in these regions.

Published by Dillon Press,
A Division of Simon & Schuster,
299 Jefferson Road, Parsippany, New Jersey 07054

First edition
Printed in the United States of America
10 9 8 7 6 5 4 3 2 1

Table of Contents

African Kingdoms

Note: Dates marked with an * are approximate.

3000 B.C.   A.D.   **800**   **1000**   **1200**

3000 B.C.	Babylonians trade with East Africa and invent writing system
1501–1447 B.C.	Queen Hatshepsut reigns in Egypt
500 B.C.–A.D. 1500	Bantu dispersal over Africa
0	Birth of Christ
***A.D. 100**	*Periplus of the Erythraean Sea* written
***150**	*Geographia* written by Claudius Ptolemy
***400**	Bantu language spoken on East African coast
610	Islam founded by Mohammed
622	Mohammed's flight from Mecca to Medina, known as the *Hejira*, marks year 1 of the Muslim calendar
***700**	Date of oldest Chinese coins found in East Africa
	Sulaiman and Said arrive in Zenj
***700–800**	First Suaheli communities appear on East African coast
757	Ammu Zaid arrives on Benadir coast

886	Ibn Khordazbeh publishes chronicle
903–913	Seven Brethren arrive on East African coast
912	Al-Masudi travels from Oman to land of Zenj
943	Ibn Haukal publishes maps of East Africa
975	Sultan Hasan ibn Ali arrives in Zenj
***1000**	Mogadishu founded
1170–1188	Sultan Sulaiman al-Hasan ibn Daud reigns in Kilwa and breaks Mogadishu's hold on gold trade
1200	Shirazi Muslims move south to Zanzibar and other islands

1204–1885	History of Paté recorded in *Paté Chronicle*
Late 1200s	Kintu becomes first king of Buganda
1355	Ibn Battuta publishes book about his world travels
1368–1644	Ming dynasty rules in China
1413	East African ambassadors travel to China
1415	Prince Henry of Portugal (Henry the Navigator) crusades in North Africa
1420–1447	Kimera, second king of Buganda, reigns
1453	Turks capture Constantinople
1483	Portugese arrive in kingdom of Kongo, now Angola
1492	Christopher Columbus reaches Americas
1498	Vasco da Gama sails around Cape of Good Hope to India
1505	Francisco D'Almeida sacks Mombasa
1580	Spain annexes Portugal
1586	Ali Bey arrives on coast of East Afica

1400	**1600**	**1800**	**2000**

1587 — Wazimba raids on East African coast

1591 — First English ship arrives in Zanzibar

1593 — Portuguese start to build Fort Jesus in Mombasa

1600 — Formation of British East India Company

1602 — Formation of Dutch East India Company

1657 — Dutch settle at Table Bay, Cape of Good Hope

1696 — Saif ibn Sultan sails from Oman and besieges Mombasa

1698 — Siege of Mombasa ends

1775–1783 — American Revolution

1804–1856 — Seyyid Said rules over Oman and all its territories

1807 — Slavery abolished in Great Britain

1808 — Import of slaves prohibited in United States

1832 — Seyyid Said builds palace on Zanzibar

1833 — Seyyid Said signs commercial treaty with United States

1838 — Entire East African coast under rule of Seyyid Said

1840 — Seyyid Said officially transfers capital of Omani state to Zanzibar

1841 — First British consulate established in Zanzibar

1856 — Kabaka Mutesa I ascends Buganda throne

1858 — John Hanning Speke reaches southern shore of Lake Victoria

1862 — Speke and James Grant visit kingdoms of Bunyoro and Buganda

1869 — Sultan Bargash of Zanzibar sends caravan to Buganda

1872 — Samuel Baker "annexes" Bunyoro

1875 — Henry Morton Stanley visits Buganda

1876 — Slave markets in Zanzibar finally closed by British

1877 — First missionaries arrive in Buganda

1884 — Mutesa I, *kabaka* of Buganda, dies and is succeeded by Mwanga; Berlin Conference held

1885 — German East Africa established

1890 — Second Anglo-German Treaty places Uganda within British sphere of influence

1894 — Uganda becomes British protectorate

1895 — Kenya, Zanzibar, and Pemba become British protectorates

1902 — Sir Appolo Kaggwa publishes history of Buganda

1939 — Last *kabaka* of Buganda, Mutesa II, takes throne

1945 — First atomic bomb detonated in New Mexico

1961 — Tanganyika becomes independent

1962 — Uganda becomes independent

1963 — Zanzibar and Kenya become independent

1964 — Zanzibar declared a republic; sultan banished; Zanzibar unites with Tanganyika to form Tanzania

1967 — Milton Obote rewrites Uganda's constitution; Uganda becomes a republic; all kingdoms abolished

1969 — Kabaka Mutesa II dies in exile in London

Introduction

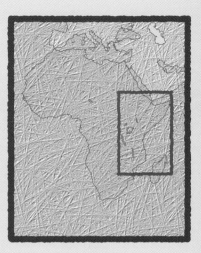

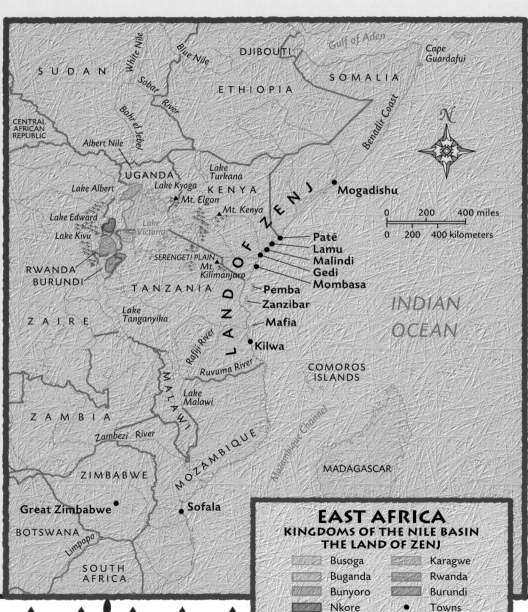

EAST AFRICA
KINGDOMS OF THE NILE BASIN
THE LAND OF ZENJ

- Busoga
- Buganda
- Bunyoro
- Nkore
- Karagwe
- Rwanda
- Burundi
- • Towns
- — Borders of modern nations

Over 4,000 years ago, the Egyptian pharaoh (FE roh)* Sahu-Re (SAH huh ray) had an inscription chiseled into the rocks along the Upper Nile. It relates that Sahu-Re sent a fleet of ships to the "land of Punt" that brought back 80,000 pints of myrrh, 6,000 pounds of silver-gold, and 2,600 trunks of a certain valuable tree.

Inscriptions on the tomb-temple of the Egyptian queen Hatshepsut (hat SHEP soot), who reigned from 1501 to 1447 B.C., also mention the land of Punt. They say that Queen Hatshepsut sent a large expedition down the Red Sea to the "land of Punt, which is called so because, in ancient times, the gods came from there to Egypt." Pictures in Hatshepsut's tomb-temple depict people of the land of Punt, living in huts made of palm leaves and raised on wooden piles. There are strange birds in the trees, and herds of cattle graze in their shade. One picture shows the ruler of Punt, followed by his wife, Ati, and men carrying gifts for the expedition. Queen Hatshepsut's ships returned to Egypt from Punt laden with gold dust, ivory, incense, precious woods, balsam, many kinds of monkeys, leopard skins, ostrich feathers, and slaves.

Where was this mysterious "land of Punt"?

Using these inscriptions and other clues, historians have determined that the "land of Punt" was in fact the East African coast, from the horn of present-day Somalia southward—though how far no one knows. The East African coast was known not only to the ancient Egyptians but also to merchants from many other regions. They brought iron tools and weapons, beads, cotton cloth, wheat grain, wine, and other goods to the coast to trade.

More than 5,000 years ago, Babylonian traders also visited the shores of East Africa. Babylon was located near the present-day city of Baghdad, in Iraq. Today the bronze or ivory horn known in East Africa as a *siwa* is a reminder of Babylonian trade contacts. Just as it was in ancient Mesopotamia, the region in which the Babylonians lived, the *siwa* is a symbol of power and authority today in the East African island city of Lamu (LAHM oo) and in many other coastal locations.

The Greeks and Romans also knew of East Africa. They called the region Azania (ah ZAH nee ah). The name may have been derived from an ancient Semitic root meaning "land of spices" or from an Arabic root meaning "non-Arab" or "barbarian coast."

Herodotus, an ancient Greek historian, relates that Pharaoh Necho, who reigned from 609 to 593 B.C., sent Phoenician (fuh NEE shun) ships to sail around Africa. Necho's expedition left Egypt via the Red Sea, rounded the tip of Africa, and returned three years later through the Straits of Gibraltar. The leaders of the expedition reported that "they had visited the land of Punt to obtain there food and drinking water."

•Words that may be difficult to pronounce have been spelled phonetically in parentheses. A pronunciation key appears on page 98.

In many coastal towns like Lamu, a siwa made of bronze or ivory is played on special religious occasions. Horns like this were also used ceremonially in ancient Babylon.

The *Periplus of the Erythraean* (er IH three un) *Sea*, (or *Voyage of the Indian Ocean*), was the first commercial guidebook to the trading centers of Azania, Arabia, India, and China. It was probably written by a Greek at Alexandria between A.D. 60 and 100. Some 50 years later Claudius Ptolemy (TAHL uh mee), also an Alexandrian Greek, wrote his *Geographia* (jay oh grah FEE ah), in which the exact locations of various Azanian ports are given. Both books refer to the most southerly town on the coast as Rhapta, which may have been located near Dar es Salaam in present-day Tanzania (tan zuh NEE uh), or in the Rufiji River delta.

Traders from Gujarat, Kutch, and Kathiawar in West India were familiar with the East African coast centuries before Europeans arrived. Skilled sailors traveling in ships called dhows (douz) used the seasonal monsoon winds to reach their destinations on the African coast and to return home to India. In the western Indian Ocean, these winds blow toward East Africa between November and March and toward the Persian Gulf and India between April and October. In ancient times, Indian traders even knew about the great lakes inland from the coast, among them the lakes that Europeans later named Victoria, Albert, Edward, and Tanganyika. The Indians' knowledge of the interior helped the British explorer John Hanning Speke, who found Indian texts excellent guides as he searched for the source of the Nile in the nineteenth century.

The Chinese called the East African coast Tsengpat or Ts'ong Pa (SAHNG-pah), their version of the word *Zanzibar*. Many Chinese coins, some dating as early as A.D. 700, as well as

> *Periplus* means "circumnavigation, or sailing around" in Greek. The word was also used for an account of a sailing voyage. *Erythros* is the Greek word for "red." The *Periplus of the Erythraean Sea* was a guide for sailors who used what the Greeks called the Erythraean, or the Red Sea, as well as the Indian Ocean. The book was 7,500 pages long!

> While Europeans struggled with two-masted ships, the Chinese were sailing vessels of 2,000 tons or more, with up to seven masts. One fleet of Chinese ships carried more than 27,000 people to the East African coast! For reasons not yet known, the Chinese shut down their sea trade after 1413 and destroyed all their ships.

Dhows still ply the Indian Ocean, as they have done for centuries. Kilwa was the farthest point along the East African coast that they could reach before the winds turned and they had to head for home.

shards of Chinese porcelain, have been found in coastal East Africa. Among other goods, the Chinese traded for African ivory, leopard skins, tortoise shell, and rhino horns, which were thought to have magical qualities.

In the ninth century a Chinese chronicler reported that "the people of this land [the East African coast] do not eat any cereals, but they eat meat; more frequently even they prick a vein of one of their oxen, mix the blood with milk and eat it raw." This practice is continued to this day by the Maasai, Turkana, and other pastoral tribes of Kenya and Somalia. The Chinese clearly had some knowledge of East Africa's interior long before European explorers arrived there. In 1413, East African ambassadors to China caused a sensation by presenting the Ming emperor with a giraffe—the first ever seen in the Far East.

From the ninth century on, Arab chroniclers such as the famous traveler Ibn Battuta and the geographers al-Masudi and al-Idrisi referred to the entire East African coast, from Somalia to the port of Sofala (in present-day Mozambique), as the "land of Zenj"

(or Zanj). They described fertile tropical islands with an abundance of food and livestock, and a thriving trade across the Indian Ocean. The Arabs coveted this land, as did the Portuguese as soon as they set eyes on it in the early fifteenth century.

In 1413, East African ambassadors to China presented the emperor with a giraffe. ▶

Arabs used the word *Zenj* for both "black"—that is, non-Arab—people and the region in which these people lived. The word may come from ancient Greek, Arabic, or Persian. The Suaheli (swah HEE lee) people of the coast believe that the name Zanzibar comes from *zenjebil*, their Kisuaheli word for "ginger," which is grown on Zanzibar. It is more likely that the name derives from the Persian term *Zenjibar*, meaning "land of the blacks."

Later, Great Britain and other European nations that were Britain's rivals in trade were to battle over the sun-drenched, palm-studded land of Zenj.

For centuries the people of the East African coast, known as the Suaheli, had been oriented toward the east—toward Arabia, India, and China, from whence came trading ships and great profits. They knew little of the East African interior, although the goods they traded were brought by Africans from the inland regions. All this would change in the nineteenth century, when the export of ivory and slaves and the import of guns and luxury goods from the West made the development of protected trade routes imperative.

The trade routes between the coast and the interior were the paths that many European explorers followed on their quest for the source of the Nile. Other explorers made their way into the East African interior up the Nile from Egypt. But all converged in the region of Lake Victoria Nyanza (nee AHN zuh), in the area known today as Uganda. Along the northwestern shores of the lake, they were amazed to find the prosperous and highly developed kingdom of Buganda. Its location in the heart of Africa—a region coveted by both the Egyptians and the British—destined Buganda to become a prime target of the colonial powers. The Suaheli peoples of the coast and the Baganda belonged to very different cultures. Yet, through trade, they became closely connected across hundreds of miles of savannah, bush, and forest. Buganda and the coast were much influenced by foreign cultures and conquerors. Islam and Christianity left their mark on both. Both endured a period of colonialism. And yet, despite these outside influences, both held on to traditional ways of life and kept their unmistakably African identity.

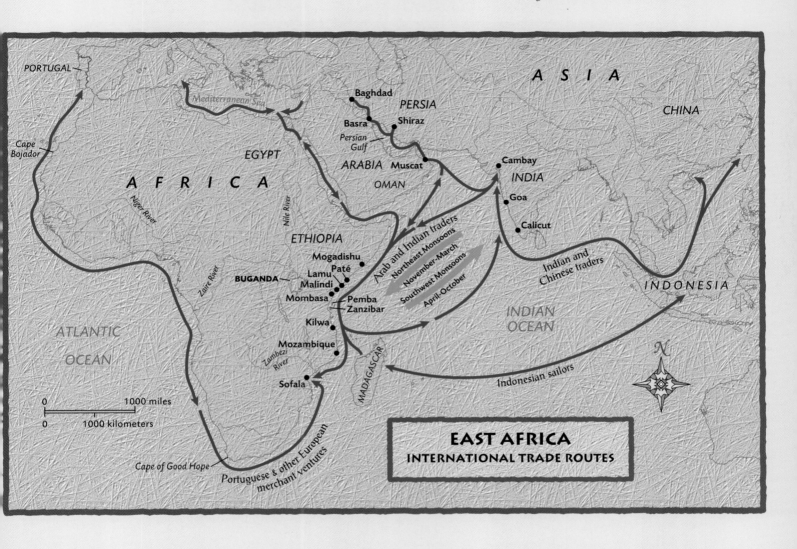

PORTUGAL

Mediterranean Sea

Cape
Bojador

ASIA

Baghdad

PERSIA

CHINA

Basra   Shiraz

Persian
Gulf

AFRICA

EGYPT

ARABIA   Muscat

OMAN

Cambay

INDIA

Goa

Niger River

ETHIOPIA

Nile River

Arab and Indian traders

Calicut

Mogadishu
Paté
BUGANDA — Lamu
Malindi
Mombasa   Pemba
Zanzibar
Kilwa

Northeast Monsoons
November–March

Southwest Monsoons
April–October

Indian and
Chinese traders

INDONESIA

ATLANTIC
OCEAN

Zaire River

INDIAN
OCEAN

Mozambique

Zambezi River

MADAGASCAR

Sofala

Indonesian sailors

N

0   1000 miles
0   1000 kilometers

Cape of Good Hope

Portuguese & other European
merchant ventures

EAST AFRICA
INTERNATIONAL TRADE ROUTES

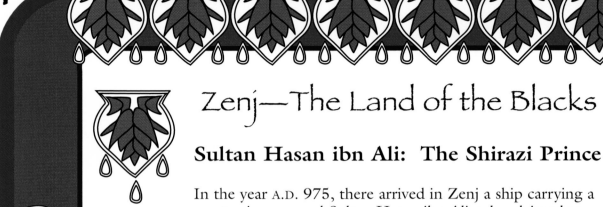

Zenj—The Land of the Blacks

Sultan Hasan ibn Ali: The Shirazi Prince

In the year A.D. 975, there arrived in Zenj a ship carrying a great prince named Sultan Hasan ibn Ali, who claimed to have come from Shiraz, in the land of the Persians. It is said that he brought with him six other ships, each conveying one of his sons.

First, these Persians conquered the city of Mogadishu, and Hasan's first son, Ali, remained as the governor of this city, ruling over the dark-skinned people who dwelled there. The second son, Muhammed, was made governor of Shougu. Baskhat, the third son, ruled Yambe (YAHM be) Island, while Sulaiman, the fourth son, governed the island of Pemba. Husain, the fifth son, became head of the Comoro Islands, and Daud (dah OOD), the sixth, ruled in Mafia. Thus did these Persians establish their rule over the black people of Zenj.

And what of their father, the worthy Hasan ibn Ali? How had it come to pass that he brought his six sons and their families and children, and his loyal followers and servants, and left his homeland to settle anew on these distant shores?

We are told that Hasan ibn Ali had a dream. In this dream he saw a loathsome rat with an iron snout, gnawing holes in the town wall. This Hasan ibn Ali interpreted as a prophecy of the coming ruin of his country. When he had made certain, through his advisers and soothsayers, that he was indeed correct, he decided to leave his country in search of a new homeland.

When Hasan ibn Ali told his sons of his plan, they retorted: "How can we go? Will the amirs and the wazirs and the council agree to your departure, which involves the breaking of the cord that binds the kingdom together?"

But their father had already made a plan. "Tomorrow," he said to his sons, "I shall summon all of you, and the amirs and the wazirs and the council. Before them all, I shall insult you, Ali, my eldest son. When you have heard me show anger, then strike me as though you were filled with rage. I shall become angry on that

Arab men in Lamu are descendants of the early immigrants from Persia, Syria, and Oman. ▶

account and make it an excuse to leave the land. In this way, if God wills, we shall be able to depart."

And it came to pass just as the sultan had planned. At the meeting, he spoke abusively to his eldest son, who thereupon struck him before them all. His father was angry and said: "I will not remain in a land where I have been insulted like this!"

The rest of his sons and all the people said: "We will avenge you and kill your son." But the sultan was not satisfied, and his people asked: "What will you?"

And he replied: "Only leaving this land will satisfy me."

The sons agreed to leave with the sultan, their father, and traveled under God's guidance to the land of the dark-skinned Zenj, where the ships dispersed, each going to the places already mentioned.

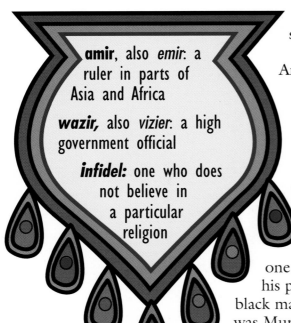

amir, also *emir:* a ruler in parts of Asia and Africa

wazir, also *vizier:* a high government official

infidel: one who does not believe in a particular religion

Sultan Hasan ibn Ali was himself in the seventh ship and sailed far south to Kilwa. When he and his followers arrived there, they found that it was an island surrounded by the sea, but at low tide, one could cross to the mainland on foot. The sultan and his people disembarked on the island, where they met a black man who was a Muslim and spoke Arabic. His name was Muriri (moo REE ree) wa Bari, and he told them that the land was ruled by an infidel from Muli who was away hunting on the mainland. He would be back in a few days.

When the infidel returned, Sultan Hasan ibn Ali arranged to meet him, with Muriri acting as interpreter. The sultan said: "I should like to settle on this island. Pray sell it to me that I may do so."

The infidel replied: "I will sell it on condition that you surround the island with colored clothing."

Hasan ibn Ali agreed to this. He encircled the island with clothing, some black, some white, and every other color besides. So the infidel agreed and took away the clothing, handing over the island and departing to Muli. But in fact, this infidel concealed his true intentions. He wished to return to Kilwa and kill the newcomer and all his following and take their goods by force.

Muriri warned the sultan, saying that the infidel was very fond of the island and would surely return. He advised the sultan to devise a strategy by which his people could remain there in safety.

So Sultan Hasan ibn Ali and his followers set to work. They dug out the creek across which one could walk to the mainland at low tide. They dug it so deep that when the tide came in, it filled the creek and did not recede again. Some days later, the infidel came from Muli and waited for the tide to ebb so that he could cross. But the water remained high and did not go down at all. Then the infidel despaired of seizing the island and was sorry at what he had done. He went home full of remorse and sorrow.

Thus Sultan Hasan ibn Ali remained on the island of Kilwa and founded its ruling dynasty. In time, his son Ali ibn Hasan became its first ruler and built there a magnificent city called Kilwa Kisiwani, or "Kilwa on the island." It had high houses with large and beautiful halls and many rooms. Each house was

surrounded by fruit-bearing gardens. The wealthy lords had clothes ornamented with gold, silk, and fine cotton, and they wore Turkish turbans on their heads. Most of them were Muslims and spoke Arabic, but they understood many other languages. Among them were exceedingly rich merchants, who had a flourishing trade in gold, silver, amber, pearls, and musk. And the people of Shiraz and those of Zenj dwelled with one another, and married, and multiplied.

Now the fearless Ali ibn Hasan, son of the great Hasan ibn Ali, proceeded to build his empire. He took his armies to the north, where he speedily conquered all the small settlements there—even the most northern town of Mogadishu—and he built his own forts and the great city of Mombasa. He went far to the south, where his forts occupied the coast, and took also Sofala, the last and most distant city of the coast. Near Sofala were to be found rich gold mines, and the dark-skinned people there also mined iron in their hills and traded their gold and iron and ivory with merchants from Kilwa. In the harbor of Sofala were ships from Oman (oh MAHN) and Shiraz and it was the last point reached by them in their journeys in the Sea of Zenj.

So did Sultan Ali ibn Hasan build his empire. From the eastern horn of Africa down to the mouth of the great Zambezi River he conquered the blacks. He brought all the existing principalities under his sovereignty and reigned from his capital city of Kilwa for no less than 40 years. May his name be praised, in the name of Allah, the Merciful, the Compassionate, for He alone knows the truth.

Putting the Story Together

The story of Hasan ibn Ali and his son Ali ibn Hasan is adapted from the so-called *Kilwa Chronicle*. This extensive history of the city was written in Arabic by an unknown Muslim scholar who probably lived in Kilwa at some time during the tenth century. The author called his book *Kitab al-Sulwa fi Akhbar Kilwa*, or *The Book of Pleasure Concerning Kilwa*.

Early Arabic chronicles of Kilwa and other coastal towns, such as Mombasa, Paté (pah TAY), Malindi, and Barawa, provide much information about the government and trade connections of the East African coast. The oral traditions of the African peoples of the region are also valuable sources of information. Usually told in the coastal language of Kisuaheli, these oral traditions have been handed down from generation to generation. Some Kisuaheli traditions date to A.D. 700, or even earlier, and concern themselves with the movements of various groups of people who migrated to the coast at different times. Some include stories about the heroic deeds of great war lords that are almost mythical. The oral traditions do not always correspond exactly with information in the Arabic chronicles. They disagree, for example, over whether it was Hasan ibn Ali or his son Ali ibn Hasan who founded the city of Kilwa and ruled for 40 years. Historians today generally favor Ali ibn Hasan.

Apart from the chronicles and oral traditions, several Arab travelers wrote about the land of Zenj. One of the oldest Arabic reports was written in A.D. 886 by Ibn Khordazbeh (KOR-dahz be), who took 40 years to write it. He comments wryly that "whoever goes to the land of Zenj, surely catches the itch." The most detailed information about Zenj is provided by al-Masudi, who traveled there from Oman in A.D. 912. His book, calculated to "stir the mind," as al-Masudi himself confessed, had the alluring title *Meadows of Gold and Mines of Gems*. Ibn Haukal (HOU kahl), a traveling merchant from Baghdad, included the first maps of the region in his book of A.D. 943. Ibn Battuta, the most famous Arab geographer, traveled to China, India, Arabia, and Africa and wrote an entertaining book about his trip in 1355. Ibn Battuta's

The Land of Zenj

"The Land of Zenj produces wild leopard skins. The people wear them as clothes or export them to Muslim countries. They are the largest leopard skins and the most beautiful for making saddles. The sea of Zenj ends with the land of Sofala, . . . which produces gold and many other wonderful things. It has a warm climate and is fertile. The Zenj capital is there, and they have a king. . . He has 300,000 horsemen.

"The Zenj use the ox as a beast of burden, for they have no horses, mules, or camels in their land and do not know of their existence. Like all Africans, they do not know of snow or hail. Some of their tribes sharpen their teeth and are cannibals.

"The Zenj, although always busied hunting the elephant and collecting its ivory, make no use of it for domestic purposes. In the land of Zenj the elephant lives about 400 years, according to what the people say, and they speak with certainty of having met an elephant so tall that it was impossible to kill it.

"The Zenj eat bananas, but their staple food is millet and a plant called *kalari* which is pulled out of the earth like truffles [mushrooms]. They also eat honey and meat. They have many islands where the coconut grows.

"The king is known as *mfalme,* (m FAHL me) which means 'son of the Great Lord,' since he is chosen to govern them justly. If he is tyrannical or strays from the truth, they kill him and exclude his seed from the throne."

—Al-Masudi, A.D. 915 from *Meadows of Gold and Mines of Gems*

work offers a great deal of information about the towns, customs, beliefs, and culture of the Zenj people.

After the fifteenth century, when the Portuguese arrived on the East African coast, writers such as the historian Joao (HAH oh) de Barros also compiled histories of the region. De Barros, who was Keeper of the Archives in Lisbon, had access to all the available documents and wrote his book, *Da Asia* (AH zee ah), in 1552. His sources were the reports of Arab historians, the chronicles, and the oral traditions. As the British, French, and Germans began visiting the east coast of Africa, they too compiled the available evidence in an effort to piece together the complex history of the region.

In addition to the written works and oral traditions, there are many ballads and songs in Arabic and Kisuaheli that relate the deeds of the great heroes of East Africa. One of these heroes was Liongi (lee OHN gee), a mighty warrior of Persian (Iranian) descent. According to one ballad, Liongi had "the strength of a giant" and ran a distance of 60 miles and back each day to take a dip in a favorite lake!

▲ The most extensive ruins of a Zenj city are at Gedi, near Mombasa. The city thrived from the thirteenth to the fifteenth century. Gedi was not a port, but Chinese porcelain and other artifacts found there indicate that its inhabitants must have been wealthy. They had built a palace, numerous mosques, and houses with sunken courtyards and walled gardens. By the end of the seventeenth century, Gedi had been abandoned. No one knows why.

The ballad also relates that Liongi's family migrated to a place near Lamu in the eighth century and gives Liongi's ancestry. Using this information, specialists have determined that the hero must have lived in the eleventh century.

Of immense value to historians are the many coins that have been found distributed over the 3,225-km (2,000-mi) stretch of coast from Mogadishu to Sofala. In 1907 an Egyptian silver coin of the first century B.C. was found near Dar es Salaam, in what is Tanzania today. A few years later, a coin of the fourth century B.C., minted during the reign of the Macedonian king Alexander the Great, was found on the Mozambique (moh zam BEEK) coast. Ancient Greek, Indian, and Shirazi (Persian) coins have also been found in the

region, as well as a few coins dating to around the tenth century, when Hasan ibn Ali arrived in Kilwa. The dates, portraits, and names of rulers stamped on these coins help to establish their origin and invite speculation about how they may have reached the East African coast.

Some researchers have calculated that there were once over 60 towns along the coast of present-day Tanzania alone. Some may have existed as early as the second century B.C. Today very few towns are left. But almost every one of them boasts ancient ruins of mosques, palaces, tombs, and graveyards. The architecture of the remains and the building materials used help archaeologists determine roughly when the structures were built. Many carry inscriptions that include dates which help order the sequence of events. Countless shards of porcelain from China, as well as glass, beads, pottery, iron tools and utensils, and jewelry, have been uncovered in these ruins. These objects can be

This copper coin is one of a horde found on the island of Mafia in 1936. Sulaiman ibn al-Hasan, whose name is stamped on the coin, was sultan of Kilwa from 1294 to 1308. He replaced the wooden houses of the town with stone ones and controlled trade in Sofala, Pemba, Mafia, and Zanzibar as well as along the coast. The inscription reads: "He trusts in the master of favors." ▶

◄ Green-glazed Chinese vases were prized because they could be stacked and transported easily. They were popular symbols of wealth and status. This vase was found in the ruined palace at Kilwa. Blue and white Ming porcelain has also been found all along the coast and deep inland, showing the extent of trade routes from Zenj to the interior.

fairly accurately dated and traced to their places of origin. They are fascinating markers on the international trade network that developed during the long history of the region.

Because there are many sources of information about the East African Coast, more is known about the early history of the region than about most other places in Africa. Nevertheless, there are still many unanswered questions. Archaelogists know of several unexcavated sites that they hope will reveal information that may help fill in the gaps in the picture of the land of Zenj.

A Coastal Culture Emerges

The *Periplus* mentions several market towns along the East African coast, starting with Opone (oh POH ne), which was probably at Cape Guardafui (gahrd uf WEE), on the horn of present-day Somalia, and ending with Rhapta. The author of the account notes that the country had no supreme ruler but that each town was ruled by its own chief. By the ninth century, there is evidence of several market towns on the coastal islands of Lamu, Zanzibar, and Kilwa and on the Comoro Islands. These towns usually consisted of many huts with thatched roofs built around a central enclosure for cattle.

Many of the market towns have disappeared. It is clear, however, that the Azanians carried on a lively trade with merchants from Egypt, Arabia, India, and China. Their main export item was ivory, prized especially in China, where it was used to make chairs for the nobility, and in India, where it was carved into fine ornaments and jewelry. The author of the *Periplus* notes that large quantities of ivory and tortoise shell were available for export from Azania. In return, he reports, the coastal Africans received "hatchets, swords, awls, and many kinds of small glass vessels."

According to the *Periplus,* traders maintained good business relationships with local people by giving them presents of wheat and wine.

The Africans also exported mangrove poles, which were much in demand for building houses in the lands of the Persian Gulf. Ambergris, a waxy material believed to be a digestive product of sperm whales, washed up on East African shores and was highly valued by foreign traders as an ingredient of scent. Slaves captured in the interior were also exported, to the salt mines of Basra and to plantations north of the Persian Gulf. East African traders also exported gold, which they obtained on the sea and overland routes leading to the gold-mining regions south of the Zambezi River, in what is Zimbabwe today.

No one really knows who the people of ancient Azania were, however, or where they originally came from. The *Periplus* says only that they were "tall," not what race they were or what language they spoke. In his *Geographia,* Ptolemy reports that "dark-skinned people" occupied the East African coast as far south as where Mozambique is today. Most probably the people of Azania were Bantu who had migrated with many other groups from regions farther west and north.

We do not know exactly when the Bantu arrived on the coast, but by the fifth century A.D., the coastal people were speaking a Bantu language. They had probably taken over the preexisting small fishing and hunting communities they had found and had learned fishing techniques from their inhabitants. They used dugout canoes and small sailboats made of planks tied together with lengths of coconut fiber. This boat design suggests that they may have had contact with Indonesians, island people from Asia who colonized the island of Madagascar off the East African coast in the early centuries A.D.

Islam Brings New Contacts

The religion of Islam was founded in A.D. 610 by a prophet named Mohammed, who lived in the Arabian city of Mecca, on the east

Historians invented the term *Bantu* to refer to the many groups of African people who moved south at intervals between 500 B.C. and A.D. 1500 from an area believed to be near present-day Cameroon. As they spread out over the continent, they settled in different areas and developed various lifestyles. Almost 400 languages evolved from their original tongue, and though these languages are now very different from one another, they have some similarities. Changes in the Bantu languages have enabled linguists to trace the paths of these wandering peoples. The word *Bantu* means "people" and derives from the common word *ntu* (n TOO), meaning "person," to which the plural prefix *ba-* has been added.

coast of the Red Sea. Mohammed had visions in which the angel Gabriel came to him and dictated various laws and traditions. These were eventually collected in the Quran (kuh RAN), the holy book of Islam. The word *Islam* means "submission to the will of Allah (God)," and those who practice Islam are known as Muslims or Mohammedans.

By A.D. 622, established religious leaders in Mecca had begun to see the new religion taught by Mohammed as a threat, and Mohammed had to flee to the nearby city of Medina.

Mohammed's flight to Medina is known as the Hejira and marks the first year of the Muslim calendar—A.H. 1. By A.D. 630, Mohammed had gathered a large following. He attacked and captured Mecca, making it the capital of an Islamic state that eventually ruled the entire Arabian Peninsula.

Only a hundred years after Islam's founding, more than half the total population of Asia and Europe was Muslim. Islamic armies fanned out from Arabia, conquering all of North Africa and the Middle East and penetrating deep into West Africa. They

People still use small boats to fish among the coral reefs and mangrove swamps of the coast. ▶

were soon followed by scholars and merchants. Their drive to spread the Islamic religion and to find new homelands more fertile than the deserts where they lived took them across the Sahara, along the Niger River, up the Nile, through the Red Sea, and along the East African coast to the land of Zenj.

The Arabs brought with them not only their beliefs but also their tremendously advanced learning in mathematics, science, architecture, astronomy, geography, and medicine. They brought the Quran and other books and introduced literacy to places where there had previously existed only oral traditions. They were able to communicate and trade with Arabic-speaking contemporaries in India, Persia, Egypt, other regions of Africa, and even southern Spain and Portugal.

Arab Immigrants

According to the oldest Kisuaheli oral traditions, the first Muslims to arrive in the land of Zenj were refugees from various Muslim regions. Mohammed left no successor and after his death, different groups of Muslims could not agree on who should be the spiritual

leader, or caliph (KAY lihf) of all Muslims. Those who rose up against the elected caliph were ruthlessly persecuted and forced to flee.

At that time the caliph ruled over a vast empire that included Arabia, North Africa, Egypt, and Turkey. The first refugees fled from Syria around A.D. 700. The Syrian refugees could have gone to India, where there were a few Muslims. But they chose Zenj, which was easier to reach than India and which was well known to them through trade. Most important, it had no ruler. Led by the Syrian prince Malik bin Muriani, the newcomers formed a small state on the coast near the island of Lamu. They were soon joined by a group of Mesopotamians who had also rebelled against the caliph.

The oral traditions then continue with a detailed description of the flight of Sulaiman (SOO lay mahn) and Said (sah EED), two Arabian sheiks from Oman who had also been persecuted by the caliph and who also arrived in Zenj sometime around A.D. 700. Sulaiman and Said had heard that the islands of Zenj were wonderfully fertile and that the Arabs and Persians living there did no manual work at all but employed hundreds of slaves to do it for them. They had also heard that "this country was immensely rich in ivory, tortoise shell, leopard skins, fruit, spices, fine kinds of wood, fish, and every kind of animal."

The sheiks and their followers settled on the island of Paté. There they married native women and kept concubines. The population grew rapidly, and the sheiks built a fortified castle whose ruins still stand today. Their settlement soon developed into an important commercial center, which, the tradition tells us, "the wisdom of Sulaiman ruled and the courage of Said protected."

In A.D. 757 another group of Arab refugees, called the Ammu Zaid (ah MOO zah EED), or "people of Zaid," came to East Africa, migrating from the Yemen region and settling on the northern, or Benadir, coast of present-day Somalia. The Ammu Zaid eventually conquered the Benadir coast and established a small but strong and warlike state there. Their capital is believed to have been at or near Mogadishu.

Next in the long line of refugee immigrants to the East African coast were the fabled Seven Brethren of El Hasa, the capital of a state in what is now southern Iraq, near the Persian Gulf. Sometime between A.D. 903 and 913, these Muslims of El Hasa arrived on the coast of Africa with a well-armed following in three large ships. They ransacked every town on the Benadir coast and had soon conquered all of Zenj as far south as Mombasa. On their way they drove the Ammu Zaid into the interior and established their own cities and states in Mogadishu and Barawa, among other locations. Barawa still has seven clans that claim descent from the Seven Brethren. In the interior the Ammu Zaid intermarried with native peoples. To this day, a tribe in Somalia, claiming to be descendants of these early immigrants, proudly calls itself Ammu Zaid.

An old story relates that when the Seven Brethren arrived in Mogadishu, they found a flock of sheep resting in the shade of some trees near a fresh spring. The Seven Brethren killed the shepherds, captured the sheep, and built a fortified town on this pleasing spot. They called the town Makdashau (mahk DAH shou), or Mogadishu—"the place where the sheep were resting."

The Seven Brethren exercised a strong influence on the coastal peoples. Within a few decades, they had converted almost the entire coastal population to their branch of Islam. The Seven Brethren were Sunni Muslims.

They accepted the caliphs who were chosen as successors to Mohammed. Members of the other branch of Islam, who are known as Shiites, rejected the elected caliphs. The Seven Brethren and their descendants were to remain in power until the arrival some 70 years later of the great Shirazi leader Sultan Hasan ibn Ali.

The Suaheli Culture

While the indigenous people of Zenj had certainly established the coastal settlements and far-flung trade networks, the Arab influence in the area remains powerful to this day. Through intermarriage between Arabs and African men and women, a mixed-blood community of people developed all along the East African coast. These people were known as the Wasuaheli (wah swah HEE lee), or "people of the coast," after the Arab word *sahel* (sah HEL), meaning "coast." Today, they are usually referred to as the Suaheli. Eventually their Bantu language developed into Kisuaheli.

At first, Kisuaheli was written in the Arabic script. Today, the Roman alphabet is used.

The historical evidence shows that the first Suaheli communities appeared between A.D. 700 and 800 at Mogadishu, Barawa, Merku, Lamu, and Malindi. During the following centuries, the Suaheli population between Mombasa and Kilwa increased rapidly with the arrival of immigrants from Persia and Oman. By the late fifteenth century, Kisuaheli had become the main language of Zenj and was spoken along the entire stretch of coast between Kilwa and Mogadishu. The coastal society of the Suaheli was Islamic in culture and religion and mainly African in language and population.

> He who wants to string pearls
> must be an excellent diver;
> he who manages to succeed
> is a pearl diver, a fisherman.
> The soul is a vast ocean;
> in it there is a treasure trove
> of mother-of-pearl.
> He who is afraid of drowning,
> for him, the oyster shells
> produce no pearls.
>
> ——*Eighteenth-century Suaheli poem*

The Suaheli poets developed a rich literary tradition. These poets were famed throughout Zenj, and their works have provided historians with much valuable information about the Suaheli culture. One of the best-known Suaheli poems, by Abdallah ben Ali ben Massir, is *Al-Inkishafi*, or "The Awakening of the Soul." It has been compared to the works of European writers such as the thirteenth-century Italian poet Dante Alighieri (DAHN tay ah lee GYE ree) and the seventeenth-century English poet John Milton.

The poem describes towns that have long been lost and forgotten. One of them was Kua (KOO ah), on the island of Mafia. It had been destroyed by pirates from Madagascar in 1790. The poem led the curious to look for Kua, and, sure enough, buried in the dense bush and sand of the island, they found the ruins of eighteenth-century palaces and noble homes, carefully decorated with Chinese pottery. Another Suaheli poem describes the ruined city of Paté:

> *Nyumba kati zao huvuma mende;*
> (NYOOM bah KAH tee ZAH oh hoo VOO-mah MEN de)
> *Kumbi za msana hulia ngende.*
> (KOOM bee zah m SAH nah hoo LEE ah n GEN de)
> The cockroach whirring flits the empty halls;
> Where nobles gathered, shrill the cricket calls.

Kisuaheli Words Taken From the Portuguese

English	Portuguese	Kisuaheli
handkerchief	*lenco*	*leso*
table	*mesa*	*meza*
wine	*vinho*	*mvinyo*
screw	*parafuso*	*parafujo*

▲ Markets in the lost Suaheli towns may have looked much like this colorful marketplace in Lamu. Oranges, limes, mangoes, and fish are among the goods sold.

Today, Kisuaheli is the lingua franca, or common language, spoken throughout Kenya, Uganda, and Tanzania and into Somalia, Mozambique, and even the eastern Congo. Over the centuries, Arabic, Turkish, Hindi, Portuguese, Malay, German, and English words have been added to the earlier Bantu language. Like a timeless mirror, Kisuaheli reflects the many cultures that have influenced East Africa.

PATÉ

Trade—Power and Prosperity

Bakiumbe: The Traitor of Manda

Over the years, the island town of Paté conquered many other towns along the coast, and they paid allegiance to Paté. Now the sultan of Manda, when he saw the kingdom of Paté had become great, wished to place a governor over these towns, for they had once come under his family's rule. But the people of Paté did not agree to this, and so trouble arose between them. It became so bad that when the northeast monsoon was blowing, if a man was building a vessel in Paté harbor and hammered a nail to drive it into a plank, an order came from Manda: "The master is sleeping; do not make noise."

Eventually, war arose between the people of Paté and those of Manda, and they fought together for many days. One day, after a space of time had elapsed, the elders of Manda were sitting in council, every tribe with its representative. One of their head men, Bakiumbe (bah kee OOM be), was not present, however, for he had gone out to sea fishing and they had not told him that there was to be a meeting.

So all the elders except Bakiumbe assembled. Someone said: "Let us wait." But others said: "There is no need to wait for him. Our words are not for fisher folk, but for elders."

So they transacted their business, and when Bakiumbe returned from fishing, he was told of this matter by his relations, for he was the chief of the fisher clan. Then he said to the members of his clan: "These men have treated us fishermen as lowly folk unto slaves, and we are all as well bred as they, save that everyone follows his calling. This one hoes, another is a blacksmith, and another is a palm tapper. This is our town, and everyone has his house, his property, and his dependents. I will make a plan that I may pay back this insult so that even those who come after us will never scorn a man again."

Now Bakiumbe took his canoe and went over to Paté and demanded a private audience with the sultan who ruled there. Then he said to him: "I wish to give you this land of Manda without trouble or war and with but little expense. Will you follow my advice?"

"I will agree," said the sultan of Paté. "But for what reason do you desire to break up your country in which are your children and your property? Tell me your reason, that I may see for myself whether it be true or false."

Then Bakiumbe related to the sultan the story of how he had been insulted by the elders of Manda. And the sultan knew that Bakiumbe would keep his word, for he was a man seized by anger, and when a man is seized with anger, he loses all wisdom.

Bakiumbe said: "I will ask you to give me ambergris. Whenever I ask for it, I want you to give me the amount I ask for. About the third or fourth time that you give it to me, I will give you the town of Manda."

So the sultan consented and gave Bakiumbe the ambergris he required. Bakiumbe set out, and when he arrived at Manda it was late at night. He knocked at the gates, but because of the war with Paté, they were closed at night, and the officer would not open them. So Bakiumbe slept outside the

gates, and the next morning when they were opened, he went to the sultan of Manda and gave him the ambergris.

The sultan was mightily pleased, for he prized ambergris above all else. "If you find any more," he said to Bakiumbe, "bring it to me and I will treat you very well."

Bakiumbe said: "I want permission to enter the gates at whatever time I may come, and you must tell your doorkeeper to open to me. And whatever I find I will bring to you, for you are my master and my sultan and for whatever you give me, I will rejoice exceedingly."

The sultan of Manda agreed. After about one month, Bakiumbe again appeared before the sultan of Manda with a large basket full of ambergris. Then he waited another month before arriving again with ambergris. After that, he waited for two months and again brought a gift of ambergris to the sultan of Manda. Each time, he came at night and knocked on the town gates, and the nightwatch let him in.

After this, he went to the sultan of Paté and said to him: "Make ready, for the work is finished. Tomorrow morning at two o'clock I will come to fetch you. Have soldiers ready. A few I shall take myself, and many must follow behind me."

At two o'clock in the morning, Bakiumbe went to Manda with the soldiers and knocked on the gates. As usual, the soldier on duty opened the gates to let Bakiumbe in. Bakiumbe and his soldiers rushed through the gates and killed the guard. They ran to the sultan's palace while other soldiers seized the other gates of the city. When the sultan heard Bakiumbe's voice, he was pleased, believing that he was about to receive another gift of ambergris. He commanded

the guard to open the palace gate, upon which Bakiumbe and his soldiers rushed in and killed the sultan and everyone else in the house.

Hearing the commotion, the people of Manda woke up and tried to flee through the gates, but these were already taken. So when dawn came, they found themselves prisoners within their own city, with no possibility of escape. The soldiers of Paté seized as prisoners both men and women, and all their property, silver, and gold, and thus it was that they conquered the country of Manda in one day. The people of Manda had many gold ornaments, and the conquerers from Paté took prisoners and property back with them to their city and thus obtained much wealth.

As for Bakiumbe, when he went to the sultan of Paté to receive his reward, the sultan said that he was too clever to be allowed to live. Might he not one day betray Paté as he had betrayed Manda? Bakiumbe, the lowly fisherman, was unable to enjoy his revenge, for he was executed. To this day, however, if there is an assembly, people will say: "Do not leave out one man from amongst our people, for he is our brother even though he is a lowly person."

Paté

The Rise of the Suaheli States

Paté is an island located off the northern coast of present-day Kenya. The story of Bakiumbe is adapted from the *Paté Chronicle*, which begins in 1204 and continues until 1885. This chronicle, which exists in several versions, is considered to be the richest and most detailed of the various coastal histories. It contains many wonderful stories, most of which arose from the memory of an individual named Bwana (Mister) Kitini. Bwana Kitini was a direct descendant of the Paté royal family and dictated his stories to the British historian G.S.P. Freeman-Grenville in 1962. Although it was said that Bwana Kitini was "a teller of tales" and could not be relied on for historical accuracy, his material remains the main source of information about early Paté, which rose to become an important center of trade.

While many of the southern towns were directed toward trade with the East, the northern towns, including Paté and Manda, seem to have had strong trade connections with Egypt. New routes had been developed that connected the Indian Ocean via Egypt to Venice, the major commercial center of Europe at the time.

Throughout the twelfth century, Christian armies fighting the Muslims had taken their crusades all along the North African coast and deep into Muslim territories. They had opened up new trade routes between East and West that helped the towns along the East African coast to meet the rising demand for gold and ivory among the nobility of medieval Europe, India, and Egypt. At the same time, inland settlements in East Africa had developed the mining and smelting of iron to a high degree. African iron was superior to Indian iron and was exported as a raw commodity. In India it was fashioned into tools and weapons that were often exported back to Africa. Large profits from the iron trade were made, especially in Malindi and Mombasa. From India, ships also brought beads, cottons, and silks to Malindi, Mombasa, and Kilwa. In exchange, they received ivory and gold, brought from mines far to the south in what is now Zimbabwe. According to one smug report, the merchants received so much gold that they departed "well pleased."

The arrival of the Arab immigrants from Persia, Syria, and Oman boosted the East African economy. Trade

The silver bracelets and anklets worn by this elderly resident of Paté were made locally. Their designs were brought from India and the Middle East with the lively sea trade of past centuries. The gold earrings and earplugs, ornaments that may date to the sixteenth century, are traditionally worn by Paté women, who shave their heads to show off their jewelry. ▶

became increasingly lucrative, encouraging more Arabs to migrate to the East African coast and attracting other Arab merchants to trade in the area. Between the tenth and eleventh centuries, some of the coastal communities grew prosperous. Mosques were built, many African leaders converted to Islam, and trade flourished. Wealthy merchants built rectangular houses of coral stone, and some of them even began to mint their own coins. By the fifteenth century, there were 40 to 60 towns along the coast between Kilwa and Mogadishu. Some settlements were tiny, consisting of only a few stone houses and a mosque. Others, like Mogadishu, Lamu, Paté, Mombasa, Malindi, and Kilwa, had many stone houses, became quite large, and survive to this day.

Kilwa—Pearl of the Indian Ocean

By the thirteenth century, some Suaheli Muslims from the north had migrated south to settle on the islands of Zanzibar, Mafia, Pemba, and Kilwa and on the Comoro Islands. They founded new Muslim towns and dynasties and called themselves the Shirazi, tracing their ancestry all the way back to Ali ibn Hasan, the great Persian prince of Shiraz.

Until then, the gold trade with Sofala, far to the south, had been controlled by merchants in Mogadishu, one of the most northerly settlements, founded in about A.D. 1000. Mogadishu was larger and more culturally developed than all the other towns. But Kilwa was the farthest point south that ships sailing with the monsoons could reach before they had to turn back. Thus it was ideally located as a midpoint on the long route from the southern gold mines to Mogadishu in the north.

The newly settled Shirazi merchants at Kilwa set out to break the Mogadishu stranglehold on the gold trade. They sent their ships south and expanded the small trading town of Sofala. Now, instead of transporting their gold all the way to Mogadishu, the peoples of the interior brought their gold to Sofala, and from there it was shipped to Kilwa. Ships from the East used the monsoons to reach Kilwa, thus bypassing the more northern coastal towns. With the monopoly over the immensely profitable overseas trade in gold from southern Africa firmly in its hands, Kilwa became by far the most important of the coastal towns of the time.

Those who came to Kilwa were favorably impressed. Visiting the city in 1355, Ibn Battuta wrote: "Kilwa is a large coast city. . . . It is one of the most beautiful and well-constructed towns in the world, and the whole of it is elegantly built. The roofs are built with mangrove poles. The sultan of Kilwa makes constant invasions into the land of Zenj, attacks them, and takes one-fifth of the war booty, which part he dictates to Allah according to the prescription of the Quran."

A German traveling with a Portuguese expedition in 1505 observed: "The town of Kilwa lies on an island round which ships of 500 tons can sail. The island and town have a population of 4,000

A minaret in Lamu towers over the coast. Lamu was one of the main markets for ivory and for mangrove poles, which were used for building. ▼

people. There are sweet oranges, lemons, vegetables, small onions, and aromatic herbs. There are many fat beasts, oxen, cows, sheep and goats, and also plenty of fish."

In 1518 the Portuguese trading agent Duarte (doo AHR te) Barbosa described Kilwa as "a Moorish town with many fair houses of stone and mortar, with many windows, very well arranged in streets, with many flat roofs. The doors are of wood, well carved, with excellent joinery. Around the town are streams and orchards with many channels of sweet water." The people of Kilwa, according to Barbosa, were "finely clad in many rich garments of gold and silk, and cotton, and the women as well; also with much gold and silver in chains and bracelets, which they wear on their legs and arms, and many jeweled earrings in their ears."

A Portuguese accountant described in detail how business was done in Kilwa.

Arab woodcarvers decorated doors with elaborate designs. Today these massive, hand-carved doors are extremely valuable. ▼

He noted that any merchant who wished to enter the city paid one gold mitcal (one eighth of an ounce of gold) for every 500 pieces of cloth that he brought in, no matter what its quality. The king then took two thirds of the merchandise, leaving the trader with one third. This was then reevaluated, and the merchant was charged 30 mitcals for every 1,000 mitcals of value. Only then could the trader leave for Sofala. Once there, however, he had to pay another duty of one piece of cloth for every 7 he brought in. In addition, everyone returning from Sofala was obliged to stop again at Kilwa. There he had to pay the king 50 mitcals of gold for every 1,000 gold mitcals he carried.

With such heavy taxes, it is no wonder that the city became exceedingly wealthy! Clearly, however, the profits to be made by merchants must have far exceeded what they had to pay in duties in order to make

The vaulted architecture of the ruined mosque at Kilwa testifies to the great wealth of its sultans. ▶

their perilous journeys across the Indian Ocean worthwhile.

For 200 years, Kilwa was considered "the queen of the Indian Ocean"—the pearl among all the coastal cities. By the late fourteenth century, however, its prosperity began to decline, perhaps because of the brief rise to power of Paté, to the north. Only the ruined mosque at Kilwa remains as a testament to the city's past glory.

Day-to-Day Life on the Coast

Although the land of Zenj is often referred to in old accounts as a kingdom, the coastal towns never actually united under one leader to form a kingdom or even a federation of states. Each town had its own rulers, or sultans, who sometimes conquered neighboring areas for short periods. On the whole, however, the towns functioned independently, though their political, economic, and cultural structures were similar.

At the very top of the social ladder were the ruling classes, which included the sultans, along with their families and relatives, and government officials and advisers and the

merchants. Most of these people were Arabic- and Kisuaheli-speaking Muslims who claimed descent from the Arabian and Persian immigrants of earlier centuries.

The sultan placed heavy duties on all imports and exports and even on goods simply passing through the town. Profits were so high, however, that merchants did very well despite the taxes and amassed great wealth. They had elaborate stone houses and palaces in which they entertained visiting merchants from abroad. They wore sumptuous robes of the finest Indian silk and cotton and ate their meals off Chinese porcelain. On their estates they grew fruit, vegetables, cotton, and millet. They also had factories where cotton cloth and glass and shell beads were made. These were needed for trade with the interior.

Beneath the ruling classes were the Kisuaheli-speaking Muslim Africans who made up the bulk of the population. They were artisans, minor officials, clerks, and the captains of the ships that sailed up and down the coast. At the bottom of the social ladder were the

◀ In a typical Lamu house, Suaheli women traditionally keep their imported Chinese bowls and plates in niches carved in the walls. In this home of a wealthy family, a servant cares for the precious porcelain.

slaves. The slaves were non-Muslim Africans bought or captured in the interior. They labored on the estates and as servants in the wealthy households of the ruling classes.

Although there was intense rivalry between the coastal towns for trade, their relationships with each other were fairly peaceful. The towns also tried to

During the thirteenth century, Marco Polo, the son of an Italian merchant, traveled from Venice across the world known to Europeans to India, China, and the Far East. In the East, he became the first European to taste pepper and brought some back to Europe. In Europe, pepper was considered so valuable that peppercorns were counted out one by one and used as money.

maintain good relations with the peoples of the interior. These Africans brought ivory, gold, and other goods to the coast and received beads, cotton, pottery, and other luxuries in return.

Expansion of Indian Ocean Trade

Trade across the Indian Ocean reached a peak between the late fourteenth and late fifteenth centuries. In 1453 the Turks captured the city of Constantinople (Istanbul), which commanded the great east-west trade routes between Asia and Europe. It was along these routes that spices, silks, and other luxury goods from the East had been transported to Europe. The routes passed through the Mongol Empire and were kept safe by its armies. When the empire began to crumble during the late fourteenth and early fifteenth centuries, however, highway robbers made the overland trade routes extremely dangerous. In addition, the Turks closed some of the routes and imposed such heavy duties on merchants using others that trade was no longer profitable. Finding new routes to the East, and avoiding the powerful Islamic states, became a priority for Europeans.

When the Asian routes closed, new trade routes were developed and ancient ones reopened, which linked the Persian Gulf with the Black Sea and with the Mediterranean. In Europe the demand for gold and ivory remained constant, but, in addition, people now wanted every kind of spice they could get. Pepper was considered almost as valuable as gold. Ginger, nutmeg, cloves, and many other spices were used to keep meat from spoiling and to enhance its taste. Most of these spices came from India and the Far East, and trade across the Indian Ocean expanded rapidly.

These developments brought even more trade to the East African coastal towns of Zenj, and they boomed. Soon, stone houses replaced mud huts in the towns, and their populations swelled as many people from the tiny coastal villages sought their fortunes in the towns.

It was this international situation that sparked European exploration. As the

Vasco da

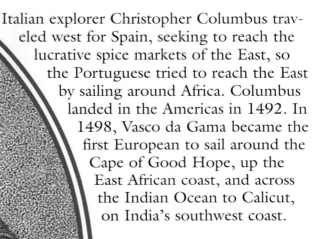

Italian explorer Christopher Columbus traveled west for Spain, seeking to reach the lucrative spice markets of the East, so the Portuguese tried to reach the East by sailing around Africa. Columbus landed in the Americas in 1492. In 1498, Vasco da Gama became the first European to sail around the Cape of Good Hope, up the East African coast, and across the Indian Ocean to Calicut, on India's southwest coast.

Vasco de Gama's arrival in the land of Zenj marked a turning point in the history of the region. His route around Africa was open to all comers. The coastal towns had previously dealt exclusively with powers from the East. Now they faced new rivals: the powers of the West.

◄ Vasco da Gama arrived in the land of Zenj in 1498. His reports of the thriving trade there brought Portuguese fleets determined to conquer the region and capture the trade.

Gama

1505

The Portuguese—
Christian Conquerors

Dom Francisco D'Almeida:
The Sack of Mombasa

In the year 1505, on 25 March, Tuesday, the Feast of the Annunciation of Our Lady, Dom Francisco D'Almeida (dahl MAY dah) sailed with a fleet of 20 vessels. There were 14 large men-of-war and 6 caravels. They rounded the Cape of Good Hope on 20 June, and on 22 July they anchored off Kilwa, and soon they had raised the flag of Portugal upon the palace walls and plundered the town of all its merchandise and provisions.

On 9 August the ships left Kilwa for Mombasa, 60 leagues up the coast. The Moors of Mombasa had built a strongpoint with many guns at the entrance of the harbor, which is very narrow. When the Portuguese entered, the first ship, which was under the command of Gonzalo de Paiva and was going in front to explore the channel, was fired on by the Moors from both sides. The Portuguese promptly replied to the fire, and with such intensity that the gunpowder in the Moor's strongpoint caught fire. It started burning and the Moors fled, thus allowing the whole fleet to enter and lie at anchor in front of the town. And on that day the town was bombarded with all the guns on the ships, while the guns of the town replied to the Portuguese fire.

The first night the fleet arrived in Mombasa there came out on the shore a Spanish Christian who was living there, a gunner by profession and a convert to Islam. He told the Portuguese to go away and that Mombasa was not like Kilwa—that is, they would not find people with hearts that could be eaten like chickens, as they had done in Kilwa, but that if they were keen to come ashore, the people were ready to set about them for their supper.

The grand captain met with the other captains and decided to burn the town that evening and to enter it the following morning. But when they went to burn the town, they were received by the Moors with a shower of arrows and stones. Once the fire was started by the Portuguese, it raged all night long, and many houses collapsed, and a large quantity of goods was destroyed. In the harbor, there were three ships from the Indian port of Cambay and even these did not escape the fury of the attack. It was a moonless night.

On Friday, 15 August, the grand captain drew up his eight ships on one side of Mombasa. On the other side was his son, Dom Lorenco D'Almeida, with three ships. Early in the morning they all prepared their arms and had breakfast. The grand captain had ordered that all should land as soon as a shot from a big gun was fired. Thus all the boats were waiting ready on the water. When the shot was fired, all got quickly onto the shore in very good order. The archers and gunners went ahead of everyone else, all going up the steep ascent into the deserted town.

The grand captain was led to the royal palace by a Moor who had been captured the previous day. When he arrived there, one of his senior captains immediately climbed up the wall and hoisted the flag, shouting: "Portugal! Portugal!"

> The term *Moor* was originally used by European Christians to refer to the Muslims of North Africa. Later it came to mean all Muslims, whether African or Arab.

▲ Modern Mombasa still echoes Duarte Barbosa's description of 1517: "There is a city of the Moors built of high and handsome houses of stone and whitewash, and with very good streets. . . . It is a town of great traffic, and has a good harbor, where there are many ships. . . . Here are found very fine sheep, and many cows, chickens, and very large goats, much rice and millet, and plenty of oranges, sweet and bitter, and lemons, limes, pomegranates, Indian figs and all sorts of vegetables, and very good water."

They saw from the walls some 60 Moors leaving the town, all dressed in gowns and turbans. They were going to a palm grove and did not seem in any hurry. Some said that the king was among them. The Moors proceeded to this palm grove, which was guarded by more than 500 archers. These archers were all black slaves of the Moors.

The grand captain ordered that the town of Mombasa should be sacked and that each man should carry off to his ship whatever he found, so that at the end there would be a division of the spoil, each man to receive a twentieth of what he found. The same rule was made for gold, silver, and pearls. Then everyone started to plunder the town and to search the houses, forcing the doors open with axes and iron bars. There was a large quantity of cotton cloth for Sofala in the town, so the grand captain got a good share of the trade with Sofala for himself. A large quantity of rich silk and gold embroidered clothes was seized, and carpets also. One of these, which was without equal for beauty, was sent to the king of Portugal, together with many other valuables. The men also carried away provisions, rice, honey, butter, maize, countless camels, a large number of cattle—and even two elephants.

On Saturday evening the grand captain ordered that all should return to the ships in a disciplined manner, keeping watch for the Moors as they went on their way. And as the Christians left Mombasa by one way, so the Moors entered by the other to see what destruction had been done. The streets and houses were full of dead, who were estimated to be about 1,500 in number.

Now the king of Mombasa wrote the following letter to the king of Malindi:

> May God's blessings be upon you, Sayyid Ali! This is to inform you that a great lord has passed through the town, burning it and laying it waste. He came to the town in such strength and was of such cruelty that he spared neither man nor woman, old nor young, nay, not even the smallest child. Not even those who fled escaped from his fury . . . even the birds of the heavens were shot down. The stench of the corpses is so great in the town that I dare not go there. Nor can I ascertain what wealth they have taken from the town. I give you this sad news for your own safety.

And thus was the great city of Mombasa razed to the ground for the first — but not the last—time.

New Sights, New Sea Routes

In 1415, Prince Henry of Portugal had been a crusader in North Africa. While there, he had seen the huge amounts of gold, silver, ivory, spices, and other goods that traveled across the Sahara from the immensely wealthy West African kingdoms of Mali (MAH lee) and Songhay (SON gye). But no one knew where these kingdoms were. Henry determined to find them. If he could gain direct access to their riches, he could make Portugal, and himself, exceedingly rich.

Prince Henry sponsored several voyages of exploration along the West African coast. Under his supervision, a new ship—the caravel—was especially designed for ocean sailing. With improved chances of returning from their journeys, captains, crews, and navigators were more willing to risk longer voyages.

Prince Henry, known as Henry as the Navigator, died in 1460, but later rulers continued to sponsor expeditions. By 1471 the Portuguese had built a trading fort at El Mina, in present-day Ghana. By 1483 they had landed at the mouth of the Zaire River and made contact with the king of Kongo. As their ships traveled farther and farther south along Africa's west coast, the Portuguese realized that they might reach the Indian Ocean—the way to the East and its lucrative spice markets—by sailing around the southern tip of the massive African continent. This way, they could bypass their Muslim rivals, who controlled all of North Africa, the eastern Mediterranean, and western Asia. It took many voyages before the Portuguese learned how to use ocean winds and currents to their advantage. But in 1498, when Vasco da Gama triumphantly rounded the Cape of Good Hope, they saw the fulfillment of their dreams of untold wealth.

The Portuguese had little if any knowledge of the East African coastal communities. When Vasco da Gama arrived in 1498, he was astounded by the beauty and prosperity of the coastal cities, many of which were

"The seas rose towards the sky and fell back in heavy showers which flooded the ships. The storm raging thus violently, the danger was doubled, for suddenly the wind died out, so that the ships lay dead between the waves, lurching so heavily that they took in water on both sides; and the men made themselves fast not to fall from one side to the other; and everything in the ships was breaking up, so that all cried to God for mercy."
—*Gaspar Correa, 1561 Description of Vasco Da Gama's expedition around the Cape of Good Hope*

◀ For European sailors, Cape Bojador (BOHJ uh dawr), on Africa's west coast, was a nightmare. The waters there were called "the Green Sea of Darkness" because of violent currents, fog, strong winds, and dangerous shallows. Before the caravel was designed, ships had to sail with the winds. Sailors did not know how they would turn around to get home. The caravel, however, could sail against the wind. Navigators learned to sail past Cape Bojador and far out into the Atlantic on the northeasterly winds. Then they traveled due south before letting westerly winds carry them around the Cape of Good Hope.

larger, cleaner, and far wealthier than cities in Portugal. The Portuguese were astonished to find harbors full of foreign ships and sailors who could navigate across oceans unknown to the Portuguese. Da Gama duly noted the thriving trade in gold, ivory, and other goods. His reports made it clear that the Portuguese could benefit greatly by capturing the trade of the land of Zenj, as well as that of the Far East.

In Malindi, da Gama found Indian navigators who used the monsoon winds to take him to Calicut. Shortly afterwards, the region on the west coast of India known as Goa was added to the rapidly expanding Portuguese empire. It was from Goa that the East African territories claimed by the Portuguese would be administered.

The Looting of Zenj
As they had everywhere else in Africa, the Portuguese arrived in Zenj not merely as traders but as conquerors. Their brutal sack of Mombasa in 1505 has already been described. It was probably written by Hans Mayr (MYE ur), a German who traveled with Dom Francisco D'Almeida.

The Portuguese were determined to seize control of the Indian Ocean trade. Their tactic was to sail their well-armed fleets into the harbors of the more important coastal towns of East Africa. With their guns poised for battle, they demanded that the ruler become a subject of Portugal and pay a heavy tribute to the Portuguese king. Refusal meant instant attack, followed by executions, rape, and torture.

The Portuguese usually installed "puppet" rulers to govern the towns. They justified their actions as a continuation of the Crusades, the holy wars in which Christians fought the Muslim advance from Arabia. Thus the mission of the Portuguese was twofold: to seize the invaluable trade of the East African coast and to convert the people there to Catholicism.

The people of the coast could not withstand the fierce Portuguese attacks. They had primitive weapons and—more importantly—no tradition of cooperation in the face of an enemy.

One by one, the beautiful cities of Zenj fell before the Portuguese onslaught. Only eight years after their arrival, the Portuguese had seized the entire land of Zenj and gained full control of the gold trade at Sofala and Kilwa. During the same period, they had also seized the trade route to India; the territories of Muscat, Aden, and Oman; and Goa on India's west coast.

Although they were now "masters" of Zenj, the Portuguese had almost killed the goose that laid the golden egg. By seizing the gold trade in Kilwa, they had seriously damaged the economy of Mombasa and Malindi, which relied on the gold to carry on trade with Eastern merchants. In addition, the trigger-happy attacks of the Portugese on the Suaheli towns and their ruthless demands for tribute not only made them the hated enemy of the coastal people but also brought trade to a standstill. Once they realized the effects of their activities, the Portuguese tried to revive trade by allowing it to continue as it had done for centuries, but it would never again reach the heights it had once known.

By building forts in the southern towns of Kilwa, Mozambique, and Sofala, the Portuguese hoped to use force to divert trade from the northern towns. But they met with strong resistance from the Suaheli strongholds in the north. The sultan of Mombasa, for example, refused to pay tribute and continued to trade directly with Arabia and other lands of the Persian Gulf. Without even an attempt at diplomacy, the Portuguese retaliated by sacking Mombasa—not once, but twice, in 1528 and 1589.

> On his second voyage in 1502, Vasco da Gama forced Kilwa into tribute by demanding the annual payment of "money or a rich jewel" to the king of Portugal as a "token of friendship." The sultan of Kilwa agreed but stated that if he had known the price he would have to pay for this form of "friendship," he would have fled into the woods. "It is better to be a jackal at large," the sultan claimed, "than a greyhound bound with a golden leash."

The town of Sofala fueled the prosperity of Kilwa and of all the coastal towns farther north. In the early sixteenth century, the Portuguese agent at Sofala collected an annual average of 51,000 pounds of ivory, 12,500 mitcals of gold—possibly worth half a million dollars today—2,000 pounds of copper, 20 pounds of coral, some lead, and a few slaves. All of this was paid for with 7,000 pounds of beads and some cloth.

▲ Building on Fort Jesus in Mombasa was started in 1593 and completed in 1599. It was designed by an Italian architect, and built by laborers from Malindi and stonemasons from India. Its massive walls and threatening presence symbolize the violence with which the Portuguese took command of the East African coast.

In 1587 about 5,000 members of the cannibal Wazimba tribe moved northward from their homelands along the Ruvuma River. Then, though no one knows why, the Wazumba raged along the coast, "killing and eating every living thing." Three quarters of the populations of Kilwa and Mombasa were massacred, and Malindi was saved only by the fortunate arrival of armed Africans from the interior.

These events forced the Portuguese to realize that, in order to dominate the Indian Ocean trade, they would have to control the Suaheli towns in the north. In their eyes, this effort required an armed garrison strategically placed in Mombasa. In 1593 they began work on the vast fortress called Fort Jesus, whose massive walls still rise from the harbor of Mombasa. For the next 100 years, Fort Jesus was to be the center of Portuguese activity in East Africa.

CLOVES • IVORY

New Powers, New Paths

The name *Mombasa* means "isle of war," and indeed, the history of the coast after the arrival of the Portuguese is one of war, revolution, bloodshed, and foreign invasions.

The Portuguese hold on the coast, already unstable, began to weaken further for several reasons. First, there were very few Portuguese left in the region—fewer than 1,000—and they had great difficulty controlling the huge area they had "conquered." Their numbers had been reduced by disease, especially malaria, and by constant fighting. The Wazimba raids on the coastal towns had rocked Portuguese confi-

dence and cost them many lives and huge sums of money. In addition, Portuguese attempts to convert the local population to Christianity had been largely unsuccessful. Finally, and perhaps the most destructive factor of all, the Portuguese had aroused intense hatred among the local inhabitants, who rose up in rebellion at every opportunity.

Meanwhile, other developments added to the Portuguese woes. In 1580, Spain annexed Portugal, concentrating more money and manpower on its colonies in the Americas and destroying Portuguese power internationally. In 1586 a new enemy appeared in the form of a Turkish galley under the command

COCONUT • COWRIES • OIL

of one Ali Bey. Ali Bey claimed to represent the Turkish caliph and promised the people of Zenj deliverance from the hated Portuguese. With the help of the overjoyed local population, Ali Bey successfully stormed one Portuguese fort after another.

Ali Bey was eventually captured, but fighting between the Portuguese and the local inhabitants continued for decades. And at the end of the sixteenth century, other threats loomed on the horizon. The Arabs of Oman had overcome the Turks and were eager to seize power on the East African coast, and the sea route opened up by Vasco da Gama brought the English, the French, and other European sea powers hot on the heels of the Portuguese.

The Rule of Oman

In 1591 the first English ship, under Sir James Lancaster, arrived in Zanzibar and Pemba. Lancaster wrote glowing descriptions of the fertility of these tropical islands and the abundance of fruit, fish, and valuable woods. His reports prompted a group of wealthy merchants in London to found the British East India Company in 1600.

They were determined to break the Portuguese monopoly on trade with the East, and in 1602, Dutch merchants followed suit by forming the Dutch East India Company.

The English and the Dutch were Protestants. Their dealings with the native peoples of Africa were different from those of the ruthless Portuguese, and soon, coastal merchants preferred to trade with them rather than with the hated Catholic Portuguese. The Portuguese regarded their new rivals with fear and contempt and did everything possible to sabotage their trading relationships with local merchants.

During this period, the Portuguese were also losing their foothold in the Arab outposts of their colonial empire. In 1651 the Arabs of Oman recaptured Muscat, their capital and the last Portuguese stronghold in Arabia. In East Africa, this news spread like wildfire, and the local inhabitants eagerly awaited the arrival of Arabs from Oman as their new allies.

Meanwhile, affairs on the East African coast were so bad that dele-

gates from Mombasa traveled to Oman, where they begged Imam (ih MAHM), or lord, Saif (sah EEF) ibn Sultan to rescue their city before it was too late. According to the local traditions, they brought a message "full of hatred and rage, picturing the cruelties of the Portuguese in words soaked in gall . . . with tears of blood in their eyes." On hearing what the delegates had to say, the imam put his hand on his sword and swore by the glory of Allah to save Mombasa or die. His motives were not purely charitable. They were also fueled by the expectation of great profits to be made on the coast. Once again, the battle raged for control of the lovely islands of Zenj.

In January 1696, Saif ibn Sultan mobilized his fleet of 28 warships and sailed for Mombasa. In March he set up a blockade of the city and besieged Fort Jesus. Knowing that this was their last stand, the Portuguese fought valiantly. Thirty-three months later, on December 12, 1698, when the Arabs finally broke through the fortress walls, 1,000 Portuguese lost their lives. Thousands of African soldiers, civilians, and reserve troops were also killed. It was a high price to pay for freedom from the Portuguese yoke.

Despite their difficulties in Africa, however, the Portuguese had skimmed off most of the East African trade and all the gold trade from Sofala. They carried their booty in ships much faster than dhows across the ocean to India and back around Africa to Europe and the Americas. And even though their own power was declining, they contributed to the decline of the Suaheli city-states. At the end of the seventeenth century, many towns lay abandoned or in ruins. A large number of the old trading families from Arabia and Persia had been destroyed by the Wazimba raids. And the local people were torn by disputes among their rulers and between the foreign invaders.

The Omani Arabs, with no strong leadership from Oman, proved no better than the Portuguese. The Suaheli, who regarded them as blood-sucking vermin, referred to them as *viroboto*, or "fleas." The Arabs tried to establish trade relations along the coast and to install themselves in the various forts, but endless wars raged

The Portuguese dominated the land of Zenj for more than 200 years. They introduced casava and the cashew tree, both from Brazil; maize, or Indian corn, from the Americas; and the avocado and guava, both from Portugal. They improved ship design and rigging and imported many useful household articles. Using snuff and playing cards were Portuguese pastimes adopted by the local people, as was bullfighting on the island of Paté.

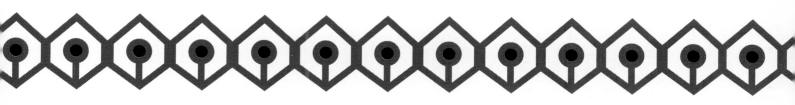

between them, the Suaheli, and the Portuguese. The Portuguese made various attempts to recapture their forts at Mombasa, Zanzibar, and other places but eventually withdrew far to the south to their settlements at Sofala and Mozambique, which they successfully defended against the Arabs. The Portuguese reign in Zenj had come to a bloody end.

Seyyid Said, International Diplomat

In Oman a new dynasty was established that took on the title of seyyid (SAY ihd), or lord. In the nineteenth century, Said ibn Sultan, a grandson of the dynasty's founder, inherited the title. He has gone down in history as Seyyid Said, a man remarkable for his foresight and wisdom. An American consul, however, described Seyyid Said as "driven by a ruthless thirst for power and wealth . . . he had no scruples with regard to the means and methods that could help him attain that wealth and power. Intrigues, lies, and hypocrisy on the one hand, slaughter of his enemies and mass capturing of slaves on the other."

Seyyid Said ruled over Oman and all its territories from 1804 until 1856.

He was kept busy early in his reign reuniting Oman, which had been torn by civil war, and building commerce and agriculture there. It was not until 1826 that he was able to focus on East Africa.

Seyyid Said arrived on the East African coast with a fleet of over 100 ships armed with 200 cannons. In Mombasa, he first had to quell several major uprisings by the powerful Mazrui family, which refused to recognize the authority of Oman. He also had to return to Oman several times to deal with rebellions there. But by 1838 Seyyid Said had subdued the entire East African coast, from Mogadishu in the north to the Ruvuma River in the south.

The lush, verdant islands of Zenj appealed to Seyyid Said and his followers, who were used to harsh desert conditions. Like the first English in the region, he noted the abundance of food and fresh water on Zanzibar and the excellent harbor. The island was close to the mainland and held a strategic position in the Indian Ocean. In a decisive move, Seyyid Said chose Zanzibar to be his

center of operations. In a small fishing village with the best harbor, he began to build a city, also called Zanzibar. In 1832, Seyyid Said built a magnificent palace there known as Beit (bay EET)-el-Sahel—the Palace on the Shore. Many wealthy Arabs followed his example, building large ornate houses nearby.

Seyyid Said had noted the international demand for spices, and with a stroke of genius he commanded the local people to plant cloves. This measure was so successful that Zanzibar eventually became the world's leading producer of the popular spice! This commercial move in turn attracted merchants, agents, and artisans from

▲ By the nineteenth century, Zanzibar was a large and thriving town with international trade connections.

India, Persia, Europe, and even the United States. In 1840, Seyyid Said officially transferred the capital of the Omani state from Muscat to Zanzibar. Zanzibar now became the commercial, administrative, and cultural center of the coastal strip. For the first time in its long history, the land of Zenj was united under one ruler.

Seyyid Said's most remarkable achievement was to establish regular commercial and political relations with the leading powers in the West. In 1833 he signed a commercial treaty with the United States which established a consulate in the city of Zanzibar a few years later. In 1841 the first British consul set up office in the city, followed shortly afterwards by French, Portuguese, Italian, German, Belgian, and Austrian consulates. All were keenly aware of Zanzibar's strategic location in the Indian Ocean, as well as the lucrative trading opportunities it afforded with the coast. In addition, Zanzibar's good harbor and plentiful food supplies made it ideal for repairing and provisioning ships.

> Seyyid Said ordered that three clove trees be planted to replace every dead or cut-down palm tree on Zanzibar. Some wealthy Arabs refused to follow the order, and their estates were immediately confiscated. There were no further objections to the rule.

In 1843 nearly 70,000 pounds of cloves and the same weight in ivory—worth a vast fortune—were exported from Zanzibar. Gum copal (a resin used for varnish), coconuts, hides from African cattle, oil seeds, and cowrie shells (used as money in many parts of Africa) were the next most profitable exports. During the 1830s and 1840s, revenues for Zanzibar more than quadrupled. The tiny island had become a competitor in the realm of worldwide commerce.

Slaves: A Profitable Commodity

The interior of Africa beyond the southern coastal towns consists of grasslands, rolling hills, and fairly fertile plains. It is possible that from earliest times there were organized trade routes across these lands. In fact, one historian suggests that from the twelfth century on, a trade route may have connected Kilwa with the gold-producing fields south of the Zambezi River and even with the great empire of Mali in West Africa. It is very unlikely, however, that trade routes were established through the merci-

less bush and semidesert that lay beyond the northern towns. Historians assume that goods simply changed hands several times from village to village until they reached the coast. There are no reports of merchants from the coast traveling in the other direction, toward the interior.

By the nineteenth century, however, distinct trade routes stretched for thousands of miles from points all along the coast to the hidden regions of the interior. The growing world demand for ivory, as well as Seyyid Said's successful commercial enterprises at the coast, had prompted the establishment of these routes. Gradually, guns and cotton manufactured in the West came to be the main imports. Ivory continued to be the main export. And along with it came the slaves—men, women, and children—who carried it to the coast and ended up on the market themselves.

The routes between Lake Tanganyika and the coast were dominated by the Nyamwezi (nyahm WAY zee) people,

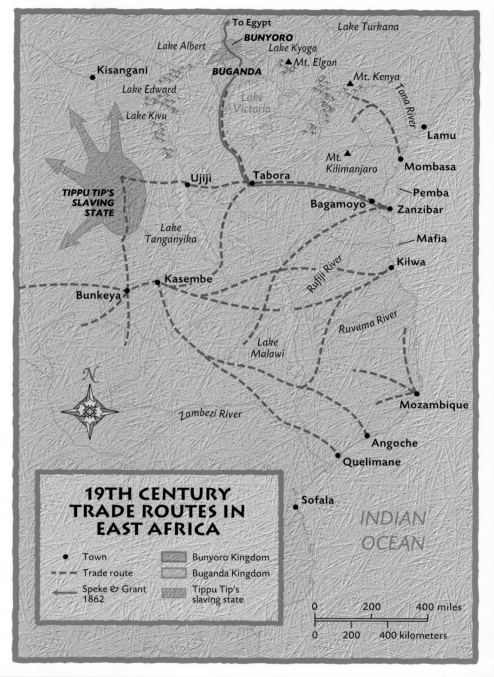

19TH CENTURY TRADE ROUTES IN EAST AFRICA

- ● Town
- - - Trade route
- ← Speke & Grant 1862
- Bunyoro Kingdom
- Buganda Kingdom
- Tippu Tip's slaving state

0   200   400 miles

0   200   400 kilometers

whose headquarters were in Tabora, 968 km (600 mi) inland, in the heart of what is now Tanzania. From there, the routes penetrated along the west side and to the north of Lake Victoria, to the west of Lake Tanganyika, and south toward Lake Bangweulu (bang we oo loo), in what is Zambia today.

Kisuaheli was the language of trade, and there were many Suaheli settlements along the trade routes. More and more, Arab-Suaheli traders dominated business, and eventually they took over the Nyamwezi settlement at Tabora.

For centuries, small numbers of slaves had been captured in the interior and brought to the East African coast. From there, they were shipped to plantations in Arabia and other lands of the Persian Gulf. In the late eighteenth and early nineteenth centuries, however, the plantation system

The most notorious of the Suaheli-Arab slave traders was Hamed bin Muhammed, known as Tippu Tip. During the 1860s he established a "kingdom" west of Lake Tanganyika. His well-armed following of over 1,000 men joined other traders there. They hunted for elephants and slaves. Male slaves carried ivory to the coast, while women slaves were concubines and worked the fields. Tippu Tip was merciless. "Slaves cost nothing," he told the explorer Henry Morton Stanley. "They only have to be gathered." ▶

"We the King of Kilwa, Sultan Hasan Ibrahim, son of Sultan Yusuf, the Shirazi of Kilwa, give our word to M. Maurice, a French national, that we will give him 1000 slaves annually at twenty piasters each and that he shall give the king a present of two piasters for each slave. No other but he shall be allowed to trade for slaves, whether French, Dutch, Portuguese, etc., until he shall have received his slaves and has no wish for more. This contract is made for 100 years between him and us."
—*Treaty between the French and the sultan of Kilwa   October 14, 1776*

all over the world expanded, and the East African slave trade, which had been relatively small, grew quickly to vast proportions.

The French had established sugar and coffee plantations on the islands of Mauritius (maw RIHSH us) and Réunion (ray yoon YON), two colonies of theirs in the Indian Ocean. At first, the French had bought slaves from Portuguese and Indian traders in the Zambezi Valley and at Mozambique. But the slaves did not last long. A large number died from overwork, harsh conditions, and heartbreak. By the 1770s the French were buying slaves from Arab and Suaheli traders at Zanzibar and Kilwa.

Men carry elephant tusks along an East African road. Even after the slave trade was abolished, people were captured to carry ivory from the interior to the coast. ▼

▲ An armed guard watches over slaves bound by chains. Rings of cloth or grass on their heads soften the load of ivory or other goods carried for hundreds of miles.

By the late eighteenth century, the antislavery movement in Europe was gathering steam, and in 1807, slavery was actually abolished in Britain. Heavily armed British ships patrolled the West African coastline—the main departure point of slaves—to prevent shipments from crossing the Atlantic. As a result, plantation owners in the Americas, among them Brazilians, whose business was exploding with the world demand for sugar, could no longer purchase huge numbers of slaves from West Africa. They looked to East Africa instead to supply labor for their plantations.

Seyyid Said himself was very involved in the growth of the East African slave trade. His clove plantations were worked by slaves from the mainland. The success of these plantations was, in fact, one of the main reasons for the sultan's move from Muscat to Zanzibar. Seyyid Said paid close attention to the inland trade routes, protecting them with armed forts and garrisons, like the one at Bagamoyo (bahg uh MOI oh) in what is now Tanzania, which was the holding place for slaves before shipment to Zanzibar. He developed Ujiji, on the shore of Lake Tanganyika, into a good harbor, and he sent his representatives far west to Mwanza (MWAHN zuh), on the southern shore of Lake Victoria. From there, the sultan's influence extended into Ruanda-Urundi, the region that is now Uganda, and even into the eastern Congo. Seyyid Said's far-reaching fame was celebrated in a popular song of the time: "When he whistles in Zanzibar, people dance on the shores of Lake Victoria."

In 1822 the British reached an agreement with the sultan of Zanzibar that prohibited the sale of slaves to Christians, though not to Muslims. When the British set up their consulate in Zanzibar, it was primarily to enforce this treaty. But it was extremely difficult to control the traffic in slaves, and traders found many ways around the new laws. Thus the East African trade in slaves flourished well into the 1870s. It has been estimated that at its peak in the 1860s about 70,000 slaves a year were exported from towns all along the coast. Zanzibar became the largest slave market of them all.

It was not until 1876 that the British finally managed to close Zanzibar's notorious slave markets. Cloves, ivory, coconut oil, rice, and copra (made from coconut husks) became the island's main exports.

> The name *Bagamoyo* means "throw your heart away"— a sad recollection of the slaves who waited there for shipment to Zanzibar.

European Explorers
By the nineteenth century, slavery had become a major political, economic,

and cultural issue among the European powers. The African slave trade began to attract the attention of European missionaries, who longed to visit Africa for themselves and end the miserable business of slavery by converting the people to Christianity. At the same time, the centuries-old controversy over the source of the Nile still obsessed explorers, and they determined to settle the question once and for all. They found plenty of financial backing from their governments. Politicians were not only interested in geography; they also needed to find exploitable resources in Africa that could replace the once-profitable slave trade.

In 1857 the English explorers John Hanning Speke and Richard Francis Burton followed the tried and tested Arab trade route into the interior. They sailed from India to the East African coast on the northeasterly monsoon winds. In Zanzibar they obtained porters for their expedition. They crossed to Bagamoyo on the mainland and from there set off to find the great lake that was rumored to exist in

the heart of the continent. The two men did not get on well and suffered enormously from the hardships of the journey. Speke decided to head north on his own, and in August 1858, he reached Mwanza. There before him stretched the sparkling waters of an immense inland sea, and—more or less on a hunch—Speke decided that this must be the source they were looking for. Ignoring the lake's African name of Nyanza, or "sea," Speke renamed the body of water Lake Victoria, in honor of the British queen of the time.

Two years later, Speke returned to East Africa, this time with James Augustus Grant. Following the now-familiar route, the two explorers skirted the western shores of Lake Victoria. From there, Grant headed north, reaching the once-powerful kingdom of Bunyoro. Speke went east, following the lake shore. There he found the great rapids and waterfalls that he had known must exist—the stirring and rumbling of water flowing out of

▲ Lake Victoria, covering 67,900 sq km (26,200 sq mi), is the largest lake in Africa and the second largest in the world. Only Lake Superior is larger. Fish are an important source of food for the Baganda.

Lake Victoria to become the great
Nile River. Speke named Ripon Falls
after the Earl de Grey and Ripon,
president of his sponsor, the Royal
Geographical Society.

On his return to London, Speke's
message to the Society was brief: "The
Nile is settled." The claim was prema-
ture, for Lake Victoria was to prove
only one of the Nile's many sources.
But Ripon Falls lay at the heart of the
great kingdom of Buganda, which
was ruled by a powerful king named
Mutesa (moo TEE sah). And it was
with Mutesa and his descendants that
future explorers and the European
colonial powers would have to deal,
for the lush, prosperous territory of
Buganda lay at a crossroad of
European interest in Africa.

John Hanning Speke was the first European to visit the
kingdom of Buganda. He died in England in a shooting
accident. Some people believed it was suicide because
of the raging controversy over his conclusions about
the source of the Nile. James Grant supported Speke's
theories and became an expert on Africa. ▶

Walumbe

Buganda—
The Hidden Kingdom

Kintu: The First King

A very, very long time ago, so it is told by those who know, Kintu came all alone into the land of Buganda. He had no other man to be his friend nor woman to be his wife, and no company save that of his only cow.

This land of Buganda was empty, stretching away to the edges of a great lake to the south and far off into the bush and the forest to the north. Now this Kintu was coarse, a man who knew not from whence he came. He had savage habits, for there was no food in the land, and so Kintu ate only what his cow gave him, even her dung.

After some time, a woman named Nambi came down from the sky to the earth. She was the first woman, and at once she took a liking to Kintu, even though he was so crude. She determined to marry him. Now Nambi's father was Gulu, the Lord of the Skies. When Nambi told her father and all her relatives that she wished to marry Kintu, they howled with laughter. How could they let their precious Nambi marry this primitive man who knew not from whence he came and ate only what his cow gave him? But Nambi insisted, and at last her father agreed that she could marry Kintu if he could pass several tests that he, Gulu, would devise.

First of all, Gulu ordered his sons to steal Kintu's cow and bring it up to the sky. When Kintu saw that his only cow was gone, he grieved and knew not what to eat. But at last, he found herbs and leaves, which he cooked and ate, and so he did not die. But one day, Nambi recognized Kintu's cow among the many cattle that grazed the lush pastures in the sky. This made her very angry, for she understood that her father and her brothers had hoped that without his cow Kintu would starve to death. So Nambi hastened back to earth where she found Kintu wandering alone, and she invited him back to the sky to find his cow. With the cow, she said, they could live happily on earth.

So Kintu went with Nambi into the sky and was overjoyed to find his cow there, grazing peacefully. He was greatly surprised to find that many people lived in the sky, each with a house, cows, goats, sheep, and fowls. And thus he passed some time at Nambi's house, enjoying himself. When Nambi's brothers saw Kintu at their house, they were angry and hurried to tell their father. But Gulu was a wise man. He could not simply throw Kintu out of the sky, for the man had done nothing wrong. After all, he had not died of hunger but had proven resourceful in his time of need. And besides, Gulu knew the will of his own daughter and that she would not give up until she had what she wanted.

◀ This unique terra cotta head was found in 1939 by builders at Luzira, on the shore of Lake Victoria, near modern Kampala. It was broken and has been reconstructed several times; but no one knows how old it is, whether it is male or female, and what its purpose was. Luzira was the site of a shrine of the Buganda Otter clan, which made bark cloth for the royal household and honored various lake spirits. The head was probably one of the sacred objects in the shrine. The knobby clay "hair" may have represented a wig, or hair dressed in clay, a common practice among Buganda priests.

So Gulu commanded his sons to build a house for Kintu so that he might stay in the sky for a while. Then they would commence with the tests that would prove whether Kintu was worthy of their sister.

First, Gulu ordered a huge meal to be served to their new guest. There were bananas and rice and the meat of many animals, all served in large baskets, along with many gourds of beer. There was enough food for a hundred people! Gulu commanded Kintu to eat it all, every last morsel, for surely the great Kintu, the first man on earth, could easily devour such a puny meal.

Kintu was left in the house, and the door was barred. Gulu's sons kept watch outside. Inside, Kintu ate and drank as much as he could, but he had barely made a dent in the great pile of food. What was he to do? Looking about him, Kintu saw that the floor of the house was made of earth, and with his bare hands he began to dig a hole. Kintu dug and dug until the hole was big enough for all the food. Then he put the food and the beer in the hole and covered it with earth and sat upon the place. Now Kintu called for someone to remove all the empty baskets. When Gulu's sons came into the house, they could not believe their eyes. The food was all gone! They searched everywhere but found nothing.

When Gulu heard of this feat, he was happy. But there was still another test that Kintu had to pass. This time, Gulu gave Kintu a

▲ Drums made music but were also used to announce births and deaths, war, the return of triumphant warriors, and many other events. There were 93 royal drums, some decorated, like this one, with beads and cowrie shells. Every chief in the kingdom supplied a drummer. Each clan chief had special drums, with special rythms for the clan.

soft-edged copper ax and commanded him to cut firewood from a rock, for he, Gulu, the Lord of the Skies, must warm his hearth.

Now Kintu was truly puzzled, for how was he to cut firewood from a rock? Surely now he would be cast from the sky without his beloved cow and without his beloved Nambi. But Kintu was not foolish, and calmly he set about the task. When he examined the rock, he saw that there were many cracks and fissures in it. When he hit them with the ax, pieces of rock broke off that looked exactly like logs of firewood. So Kintu hammered again and again at the rock until he had a large pile of rock logs, and these he presented to Gulu.

Now Gulu wished to test Kintu just one more time and sent him to fetch dew for his drink, because the great Gulu, Lord of the Skies, did not drink well water. Kintu took a pot and went off into the fields and pondered how he was to complete this task. He put the pot down and lay down under a tree to think. Perhaps he slept and dreamed, or perhaps the spirits came to his aid, for when Kintu awoke, he found that the pot was full of dew water!

Now Gulu was delighted. What a catch was this Kintu for his daughter Nambi, for he could not be robbed or cheated, so clever was he! And what fine children they would have! So Gulu gave Kintu his cow and many calves that the cow had born during her stay in the sky. And he also gave him goats, sheep, chickens, plantains, and millet—in short, everything the couple might need to establish their home on earth.

Before Kintu and Nambi could leave, Gulu warned them that they must hurry away, for otherwise Walumbe (wah LOOM be), the bringer of death, would want to go with them, and he would cause them only unhappiness and pain. If they had forgotten anything, they were not to turn back, for then Walumbe would go with them.

Kintu and Nambi set off with all their new belongings. But after a while, Nambi remembered that she had forgotten the grain for the chickens. If she did

not return for it, all the chickens would die. Kintu reminded her of Gulu's warning, but Nambi was stubborn and returned to the sky to fetch the grain. Gulu was outraged. Was his daughter then so stupid that she could not obey such a simple command? Now Walumbe would be her companion forever!

▲ This huge hut, located on a hill near Kampala in present-day Uganda, enshrines the graves of three Buganda kings. It also houses spears, shields, and other relics.

Nambi tried to slip away from the sky without Walumbe, but he was everywhere. So Nambi and Kintu returned to earth with their new companion, who left them in peace for a time. The happy couple planted their garden and had many children. One day, Walumbe returned and asked for one of Kintu's daughters to be his cook. Kintu refused to give his daughter to Walumbe. After all, he said, he might need her as a gift to Gulu. But Walumbe said that he would take the child anyway, for he would take her in death.

Now Kintu and Nambi had no knowledge of death. But soon, their children began to fall ill and to die, for Walumbe had held to his promise. In this way they learned of death, and it was with them forever, as Gulu had prophesied. But Kintu never lost his hope or his courage. He knew that he and Nambi would continue to have children forever, and that Walumbe, the bringer of death, could not wipe them out. And so it has been told, by those who know, that all of this happened a very, very long time ago.

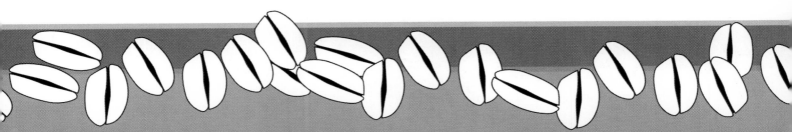

The Kintu Story

The story of Kintu is well known among the Baganda of today, in both its oral and its written forms. This version has been adapted from a story collected by Sir Apollo Kaggwa, a Baganda historian, in 1902. He interviewed elderly Baganda for his material and also consulted a Luganda version published in 1882 by Catholic missionaries.

> **Buganda:** the kingdom or state
> **Baganda:** the people of Buganda
> **Muganda:** one person of Buganda
> **Luganda:** the language of the people of Buganda

Kintu has two very important roles in Buganda lore. He is the legendary hero of a creation myth, like the one just told, and he was also the first king of Buganda, from whom all later kings traced their descent. Traditional stories about Kintu thus fall into two categories: the *lugero* (loo GE roh), or legends, and real history, or *byafayo* (bee ah FAH yoh).

The Kintu *lugero* or creation myth explains the origin of the world, its division between earth and sky, the differences between the gods and human beings, and the nature of life and death. Kintu, the hero, "conquers" Walumbe, or Death, with his promise that "his children"—that is, the Baganda people—will never die out.

The story also sets forth a code for the moral and practical behavior of Baganda men and women. Kintu, for example, is first seen as a primitive being who knows nothing of his own origins or of how to work the land for food. He must first become socialized through the rituals of courtship, marriage, and the fathering of children before he can be considered a full member of Baganda society. His wife, Nambi, on the other hand, shows a shocking lack of obedience to both her father and her husband-to-be. Her bad behavior brings trouble—including death—to the Baganda people.

Some historians claim that because of this story, Baganda women have always been treated as mere pieces of property or even slaves. Other historians note

columbus monkey

civet

Six

Baganda

When Kintu arrived in Buganda, he was asked by the local clans to help rid them of a tyrannical lord named Bemba, the Snake. Bemba ruled from a place called Nagalabi, later known as Buddo Hill. Kintu's men killed Bemba. After they had put out the fire at his hearth and buried his body, they carried Bemba's head to Kintu and asked him to become their king, or *kabaka* (kah- BAH kah). Kintu agreed and spent the night in Bemba's house. After that, he built his capital at Magonga (not far from Kampala today) and ruled for many years.

This story includes all the rituals required when installing a new king. Later kings always reenacted the fight against a predecessor in mock combat, put out the fire in his hearth, and spent a night in his house. Kintu was also, according to legend, the founder of the kingdom of Bunyoro.

that in early versions of the story it is Kintu, not Nambi, who disobeys Gulu and brings death to the people. It is very possible that the later versions of the story were influenced by the Christian story of Adam and Eve, and even by certain ideas of Islam, which preceded Christianity in Buganda by about 15 years.

In the *byafayo*, or historical stories, about Kintu, he emerges as a dynamic and capable leader who became the first king of Buganda in the late thirteenth century. Kintu may have been an actual individual, whose story has been handed down for generations; or he may simply symbolize the arrival of a conquering dynasty.

From these *byafayo* and from Baganda clan traditions, historians have concluded that before Kintu's arrival, the land along the northwestern shore of Lake Victoria was inhabited by native people living in six clans, each of which was governed by its own chief. Over time, they were joined by thirteen other clans, led by

Clans

raying
nantis

lungfish

shrike

reedbuck

▲ These glazed pots resemble gourds and were made by royal Buganda potters who received land in exchange for their exquisite work. Apparently the art of pottery was introduced into Buganda by captives from the nearby kingdom of Bunyoro.

> Each of the six native clans had a totem: the mantis, the civet cat, the colobus monkey, the bird, the lungfish, and the reedbuck. We know very little about the people of these clans, except that today's Luganda must have evolved from their language.

Kintu, which migrated from a place "east of the Nile" and settled all over Buganda. Some researchers suggest that Kintu and his followers were not Negroid, like the Bantu people, but Hamitic—that is, descended from the ancient North Africans, Ethiopians, or Egyptians. No one knows why they migrated, but, whatever their origins, the fine noses and coppery skin of Kintu and his people remained evident in the royal family of Buganda for hundreds of years.

Like the beginning of Kintu's story, the end is also shrouded in myth and mystery. It is said that unlike ordinary mortals, Kintu never died. He was filled with horror at the bloodshed caused by his violent sons and simply "disappeared," entering a forest grove at a place called Magonga. This place is now a sacred site where Kintu's spirit lives on.

The Cradle of the Nile

John Hanning Speke found one of the sources of the Nile at the great rapids he named Ripon Falls, now the site of a hydroelectric dam. Later, the explorers Samuel Baker and Henry Morton Stanley would map out the region of the lakes that the British named Albert and Edward. At last, it was understood that the Albert Nile and the Victoria Nile are the headwaters of the mightiest river of all rivers, and the entire region became known as "the cradle of the Nile."

To the west of the region lies the Ruwenzori Range, its snowcapped peaks towering over 5,000 m (16,000 ft) above sea level. These are the famed "Mountains of the Moon," mentioned by Ptolemy in his *Geographia* nearly 2,000 years ago. To the east of the Ruwenzoris, the Rift Valley snakes its way down from the north, harboring within its walls Lakes Albert, George, Edward, and Kivu. To the southeast lies the luxuriant northern shore of Lake Victoria, now heavily cultivated but still showing pockets of dense rain forest. And to the north and east, grassy savannah stretches into the arid regions bordering the present-day nations of the Sudan and Kenya. Most of the land within these boundaries is a plateau between 1,200 and 1,500 m (3,500 and 4,500 ft) above sea level. Because of its elevation, it has a pleasant climate year-round with plenty of rainfall.

The landscape of the region, with its many freshwater lakes and fertile soils, attracted many people over the course of time. They were driven perhaps by famine, disease, overpopulation, war, or the thirst for new lands. After the Kintu migration, sometime between the fifteenth and sixteenth centuries, the Luo (LOO oh) people moved south from the southern provinces of the Sudan. Some Luo colonized what is now northwestern Uganda. Others settled in what is western Kenya today. One group, known as the Babito (bah BEE toh), crossed the Albert Nile and invaded the province of Bunyoro, which hugs the eastern shore of Lake Albert. They overcame or drove out the previous inhabitants, known as the Bacwezi (bahk WE zee). The Babito founded a dynasty of Bunyoro kings and eventually built a large and prosperous kingdom.

There is still much debate among historians concerning the origins of the Luo invaders and their effect on the lands they entered. For example, Buganda, along with several smaller

The Baganda worshiped several gods and fetishes, as well as the spirits of dead relatives. The gods were worshiped in temples, which were large conical huts with thatched roofs, located on sacred land estates. Priests maintained the temples, took the people's offerings to the gods, and interpreted the words, or oracle, of a medium who lived at the temple. The highest-ranking god was Mukasa (moo KAH sah), god of healing and of plenty. His temple was on an island in Lake Victoria and hid a large meteor that was turned to the east or to the west, depending on the phases of the moon. At the annual festival for Mukasa, the king sent an offering of nine each of men, women, white cows, white goats, white fowls, loads of bark cloth, and loads of cowrie shells, for nine was the sacred number for all gifts and offerings. Mukasa's brother Kibuka was the god of war. The fire in his temple was obtained when the priest struck a rock with a tuft of grass. The fire was kept burning day and night during the reigning king's lifetime, and extinguished on his death. It was relit when the new king ascended the throne.

Some Buganda Gods

Katonda—the Creator
Wanga—god of the sun and of disease
Musisi—god of earthquakes
Kitaka—god of the earth and its fertility
Nagawoni—goddess of hunger
Walumbe—god of death
Mbale—god of women's fertility
Kaumpuli—god of plague

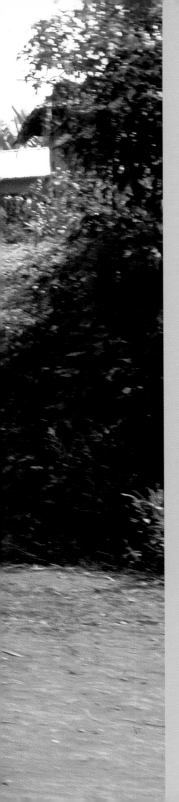

◀ Uganda's climate was perfect for growing bananas and plantains which yielded large crops with very little work. Unlike their neighboring cattle-keeping societies, the Baganda had no need to search for new pastures. Bananas supported a large population in a relatively small area. The need to defend this territory from enemies promoted the development of a strong central government. Bananas are still a main source of food in present-day Uganda.

kingdoms to the south of Bunyoro, such as Ankole (an KOH le), Burundi, Ruanda, and Karagwe (kah RAHG we), emerged around the time of the Luo invasion. Were these kingdoms formed by people organizing themselves in defense against the Luo? Or did the kingdoms develop from preexisting political systems? Whatever the case, the small state of Buganda steadily rose in size and power until it had surpassed Bunyoro, its rival to the northwest.

By the mid-nineteenth century, the Buganda kings, or *kabakas*, had become supremely powerful figures and had greatly reduced the traditional authority of the clan chiefs. Only "sons of the drum"—that is, sons of a former ruler—could aspire to the throne. They were usually selected by the *katikiro* (ka tih KEE roh), or prime minister, and the *mugema* (moo GE mah), or chief clan head. Those sons not selected were usually killed.

The *kabaka* never gave awards of land to male relatives for fear that they might develop rival centers of power. Instead, he granted estates of land to regional chiefs, who maintained their positions only through loyalty to the king, not

Before cotton was introduced by Arab traders from the coast, Baganda people made beautiful clothing out of bark. It was stripped from a type of fig tree and pounded until it was soft and flat. ▼

through hereditary claims. The chiefs in turn granted loyal minor officials control over small parts of their estates. Military regiments were established all over the region, and the *kabaka*'s spies watched over the affairs of the chiefs.

The estates themselves were worked by peasants. Some of the food and other goods that they produced, such as bark cloth, were passed up the chain of the hierarchy as a form of tribute, which always landed in the lap of the king. The *kabaka* was thus not only the most powerful but also the wealthiest man in the kingdom.

During this period, Buganda itself was in turmoil. As the *kabaka*'s power grew, so also did the fear of people around

him. Random executions and torture, used to demonstrate power, were a fact of daily life at the king's court. With fear came competition for wealth and royal favors, resulting in much violent rivalry. People supported this system because with intelligence, cunning, and political savvy any individual could advance into the higher ranks.

Adding to the confusion in Buganda were the Zanzibari Arabs, who had been bringing guns, cotton, Chinese porcelain, Indian silks, and other luxuries into Buganda in exchange for ivory since the late eighteenth century. With these goods, the Arabs brought the new ideas of Islam and the intoxicating scents of the world beyond Buganda.

It was into this changing scene in Buganda that Mukabya (moo kah-BEE yah), popularly known as Mutesa, was born and ascended the throne in 1856 as a young man in his early twenties.

Kabaka Mutesa and the Europeans
On February 18, 1862, John Hanning Speke was formally received by Kabaka Mutesa I, thirtieth king of Buganda, at his capital at Banda, a

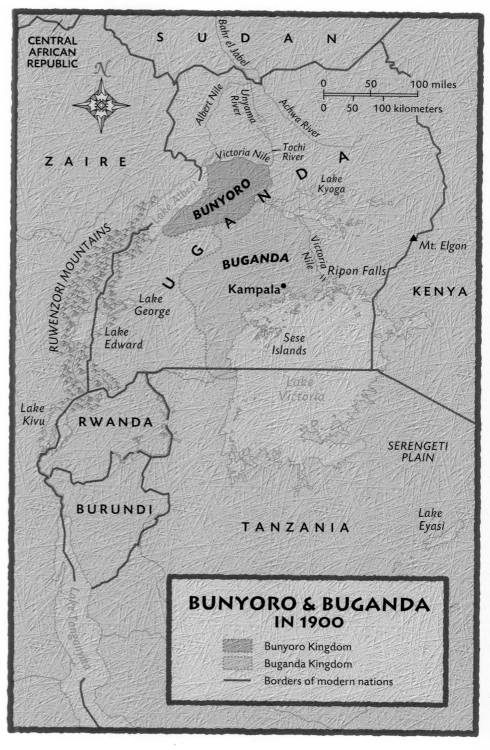

**BUNYORO & BUGANDA
IN 1900**

Bunyoro Kingdom
Buganda Kingdom
— Borders of modern nations

few miles from present-day Kampala. News of Speke's coming had preceded him, and he was received by Mutesa's dignified envoys. The *kabaka* was as anxious to meet this European stranger as Speke was to meet him.

Amid volleys of gunfire and joyous strains of noise from the court musicians, Speke was conducted to the magnificent chamber where Mutesa awaited him. The *kabaka*—a tall, slender, young man wearing flowing robes and carrying a spear—was surrounded by his great chiefs and many wives. "Everything about him was light, elegant and neat," wrote Speke. "Not a fault could be found with the taste of

◀ Speke approached the *kabaka's* palace over wide, clean roads that radiated from the capital. There were no wheeled vehicles, but the roads helped communications and trade and enabled the king to keep control over the outlying regions. Speke wrote: "The [*kabaka's*] palace quite surprised me by its extraordinary dimensions, and the neatness with which it was kept. The whole brow and sides of the hill were covered with gigantic grass huts, thatched as neatly as so many heads dressed by a London barber ..." There were often 1,000 men in the royal enclosure, busy repairing or building the houses.

his getting up." Speke also noted that Mutesa was an extremely loving husband and father. Later, however, after observing Mutesa cruelly demonstrate his power through random killings of his subjects, Speke would describe him as "vain and heartless."

Mutesa himself, tantalized by visitors and goods from the outside world, was eager to develop diplomatic and trade relations with both the Europeans and the Arabs, and news of his ambitions spread. Sultan Bargash of Zanzibar heard from Arab

Some years after Speke's departure, Mutesa, shown here with his court officers, converted to Islam. He discarded his cotton robes for the Muslim caftan and fez (hat). ▼

The Baganda eagerly traded at many well-organized marketplaces. The earliest currency was a small ivory disc called a *sanga*. Later, blue beads were introduced, and later still, cowrie shells. The cow was a standard measure of value, equal to 2,500 cowries or 5 goats. A male slave was sold for 1 cow; a female slave—who could bear many offspring—for 4. An ivory tusk was worth 1,000 cowrie shells.

traders that there were good prospects in Buganda. In 1869 he sent a caravan west to Buganda, bearing greetings for Mutesa. In return, Mutesa sent his envoys along the same route back to Zanzibar, bearing gifts for Bargash. From then on, trade with the coast increased in volume. As usual, guns and cotton were imported, and ivory and slaves were exported to the coast.

Along with Arab trade came the Islamic faith, which Mutesa adopted whole-heartedly. He learned Arabic, wore Arab dress, followed Arab manners, and observed the Islamic holy days. Most members of his court became Muslims, and almost every chief in the kingdom built a mosque. Islam was the first foreign religion introduced into Buganda, and although it did not sweep the country, it did make people receptive to new ideas and new cultures.

Speke did not stay in Buganda for long. He had, after all, accomplished his mission. Speke met Grant in Bunyoro, and the two explorers headed down the Nile to Egypt. At this time, the Egyptian ruler, or *khedive* (ke DEEV), was trying to expand his empire south into the region of the great lakes. He appointed the British officer Samuel Baker, who explored the region after Speke and Grant, to establish Egyptian rule there. In 1872 Mutesa watched with apprehension as Baker annexed Bunyoro and burned the king's capital to the ground. It

Mutesa brought about many changes in Buganda. Although he was the highest authority, he consulted the elderly chiefs in important matters of state. He allowed his subjects to practice whatever religion they wished. When cotton was scarce, only the royal family was permitted to wear it. But as cotton imports increased, Mutesa allowed his subjects to wear cotton *kanzus* (a kind of caftan) and trousers. Mutesa also, however, encouraged the sale of people into slavery, and it was only the condemnation of the missionaries that brought this practice to an end.

was not long before Colonel Charles Gordon, Baker's successor, was planning to do the same in Buganda. Fearing that their lucrative ivory trade would be siphoned off to Egypt, the Zanzibari Arabs in Buganda began to meddle in Mutesa's affairs.

Increasingly, Mutesa felt himself trapped in a situation beyond his control. By now, several Europeans had visited Buganda. In 1875 the explorer Henry Morton Stanley arrived in Buganda. He was to have a profound influence on the *kabaka*. Like Speke,

When Stanley arrived in Buganda, the *kabaka* gave him a royal reception. ▼

"In person Mutesa is tall, probably 6 feet 1 inch, and slender. He has very intelligent and agreeable features, reminding me of some of the faces of the great stone images at Thebes and of the statues in the Museum at Cairo. He has the same fullness of lips . . . relieved by the general expression of amiability blended with dignity that pervades his face, and the large, lustrous . . . eyes that lend it a strange beauty. . . . His color is of a dark red-brown, of a wonderfully smooth surface. When not engaged in council, he throws off unreservedly the bearing that characterizes him when on the throne, and gives free reign to his humor, indulging in hearty peals of laughter."

—Henry Morton Stanley, 1878
Through the Dark Continent

Stanley had come to solve the mysteries of the Nile, but unlike Speke, he developed a true friendship with Mutesa, who had changed a great deal since adopting Islam. The British explorer believed that the intelligent *kabaka* could "aid the civilization and enlightenment of a vast portion of Central Africa."

Stanley saw in Buganda fertile grounds for the spread of Christianity and the end of slavery. It was at his suggestion that Mutesa opened his kingdom to Christian missionaries, hoping that they might form a forceful buffer to the Egyptian threat from the north.

In 1877, a few months after Stanley published an appeal for missionaries in London's *Daily Telegraph*, the first members of the British Protestant Church Missionary Society arrived. They were followed soon afterward by the French Roman Catholic White Fathers. So keen was Mutesa to win European support that he even abandoned Islam for a number of years and proclaimed himself a Christian. But whatever hopes of political solidarity with Europeans Mutesa might have had were soon dashed. The two groups of missionaries were intense rivals, and the tensions between them and the Muslim community soon led to violence and bloodshed.

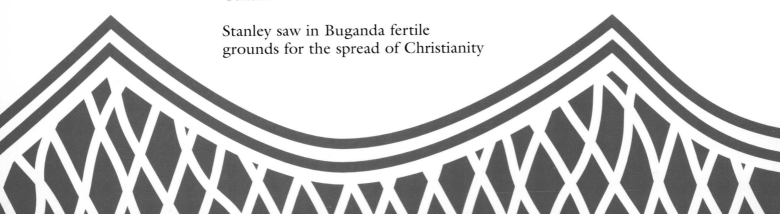

Throughout the turmoil, Mutesa attempted to steer a diplomatic course. But events in distant countries were running their course and would soon have far-reaching effects on the kingdom of Buganda. In addition, Mutesa had been seriously ill for many years, and his strength had begun to wane. Between 1880 and 1884, a series of devastating plagues and cholera epidemics killed thousands of his subjects as well as many of his beloved wives and children, including all but one of the suitable successors to the throne.

Mutesa's condition worsened. Some Arabs came forth with a "cure," but it proved fatal, and in October 1884 the great *kabaka* died. He was deeply mourned throughout the world as an extraordinary leader who had peacefully opened up his country to new civilizations and cultures. Through skilled diplomacy and tact, he had prevented the Egyptian *khedive* from hoisting the Egyptian flag on Lake Victoria. He had also built a strong, united nation with no rival in the region.

Major international newspapers published lengthy obituaries of Mutesa. They may as well have mourned the death of Buganda itself, for Mutesa's death signaled the end of Buganda's existence as an independent state. Explorers, missionaries, traders—all were but forerunners of the colonial powers that were soon to descend.

The Reverend John Roscoe of the Church Missionary Society did most of the early studies on the Baganda. The British newspapers of the time sensationalized Roscoe's findings with headlines such as "Cannibal Morals," "Queer Secrets of East Africa," "Drugged Babies," and "Wives on Loan." They referred to photographs of "strange and grim ceremonies" and of "fetishes . . . going back to 2000 B.C." The newspaper articles reflected British attitudes toward Africa at the time. Readers were thrilled by stories about cannibalism, superstition, and "primitive" people.

Epilogue

Had Mutesa lived for a few more years, he might have regretted his "open-door" policy toward the Europeans. He had invited missionaries to work in Buganda in the hope that their presence might prevent the southward thrust of the Egyptian forces. But their open hostility to one another caused suspicion and distrust in Buganda and triggered the eventual takeover of the kingdom by the British.

Mutesa had complete control over his kingdom and closely monitored the activities of all foreigners, including even the Arab traders. He had been adept at playing the missionaries off against each other and thus had preserved Buganda's religious independence. But his son Mwanga, who became *kabaka* in 1884, had no such skills. Before long, the rivalries between the two groups of missionaries and the

Muslims had erupted into full-scale war. The Muslim Baganda and their Suaheli and Arab merchant allies were thrown out and retreated to the rival kingdom of Bunyoro.

The British now felt justified in taking on the "burden" of administering the chaotic region of Uganda (as they called the Nile basin)—both to protect their missionaries and to end the slave trade. They were also anxious to control Egypt by controlling the source of the Nile, on which it depended. Events in Europe, however, would soon shape the future of the entire African continent.

Until the late nineteenth century, Britain was the unchallenged leader in the industrial world and promoted a policy that allowed all European nations to trade freely in Africa without interference from one

The Scramble for Africa

another. By the late 1860s, however, Germany, France, and the United States were catching up with Great Britain in industrial development. Their factories produced huge quantities of cloth, guns, alcohol, and metal goods that needed new markets. At the same time, gold and diamonds had been discovered in southern Africa, and it was believed that the continent held other valuable resources.

It now suited Britain and other European powers to create protectorates in Africa, areas in which they would hold exclusive rights to trade. The rush to claim such regions was described as the "Scramble for Africa." At an international conference in Berlin in 1884, Africa was divided among the European powers. They created most of the artificial nation states that exist on the continent today, ignoring the existing ethnic and political rivalries between Africa's peoples.

In 1884, Dr. Karl Peters, founder of the Society for German Colonization, arrived in Zanzibar and crossed to the mainland. He made several "treaties" with African chiefs, who understood nothing of what he was up to and "sold" their land in return for German "protection." In 1885 the German government awarded Peters a land charter, and the new territory—in the face of increasing African resistance—became known as German East Africa.

Sultan Bargash of Zanzibar, who regarded the coast as his domain, was outraged and demanded help from the British, who negotiated a treaty with the Germans. In one swift move, however, the sultan's power over the interior of East Africa was reduced to a 16-km (10-mile) strip of the 970 km (600 mi) of the coast, with the islands of Lamu, Pemba, and Mafia thrown in. Germany received Tanganyika (known today as Tanzania), and Britain—with its eye firmly on Uganda—kept what is now Kenya.

The Imperial British East Africa Company (I.B.E.A.)—a private merchant enterprise—eventually bought trading rights to the coastal strip from Sultan Bargash. It also claimed rights to Zanzibar, which was supposed to

> "You must live some time amongst the Africans to know what they really are, and what are the motives which influence their actions. Travelers pass through the land as strangers to the people, while the people are strange to them, and thus easy occasion is given for mistrust and misunderstanding. But when you really know them, are sympathetic with them, and they know and like you, your experience is far more pleasant."
>
> —Reverend Henry Rowley, 1876
> Universities Mission to Central Africa

be independent, and to the nearby island of Pemba. Germany received rights to the island of Mafia. In return for the islands of Zanzibar and Pemba, the British "gave" the island of Helgoland in the North Sea to Germany—perhaps one of the oddest exchanges in imperial history. And in a second agreement, the Anglo-

German Treaty of 1890, Britain brought Uganda securely within its sphere of influence.

From here on, things moved very fast. By 1895 the British government had taken over from the I.B.E.A. and declared Kenya a protectorate, along with Zanzibar and Pemba. Zanzibar's

Just as in the past, Mombasa today shows the influence of many cultures.▼

coastal strip in German East Africa fell to Germany. Thus, although Zanzibar was still dominated by Arabs, the sultan himself was rendered entirely powerless. During World War II, the British won Tanganyika from the Germans, and the nation became independent in 1961. But it was not until 1963, when Britain granted Zanzibar its independence, that the sultan was able to reclaim his former authority. Only a few weeks later, however, in early 1964, the sultan's regime was overthrown in a violent revolution. The African people had had enough of Arab domination. In April 1964, Tanganyika and Zanzibar joined to form the independent republic of Tanzania.

In Uganda the British initially handed over the exploitation and administration of Uganda to the I.B.E.A. They sent Lord Lugard, an experienced colonial administrator, to establish their authority in Buganda. He allied himself with the powerful, high-ranking Christians, among them Kabaka Mwanga himself, whom he "persuaded" to accept British rule. In 1894 the British government took over from the I.B.E.A. The kingdoms of Buganda, Ankole, Toro, and Bunyoro, together with other lands in the region, were combined in the British protectorate of Uganda.

The kingdoms did not submit willingly to British administration. In 1897, Mwanga staged an unsuccessful revolt and was deposed. In 1899, after attempts to regain his throne, Mwanga was captured by the British and deported to the Seychelles Islands in the Indian Ocean, where he died in 1903. Kabarega, the king of Bunyoro, who also rebelled against the British, suffered the same fate.

After years of intrigue and bloodshed, everyone in Buganda wanted peace. In 1900 the British devised the so-called Buganda Agreement. In this treaty, the British agreed not to take land for white settlement. Instead, they parceled out the land to the Baganda chiefs, giving them life-long leases. This removed the *kabaka*'s ancient right to allot land to loyal chiefs, and thus effectively broke his power. After 400 years of absolute monarchy, the *kabaka* was reduced to a mere figurehead, appointed by the

Uganda's population today consists of pastoralists, like the Karamajong of the dry northeastern region, and farmers, like the Baganda. About 65 percent of Uganda's people are Christians, with about 6 percent Muslims and the rest practicing other religions. Because of the early introduction of literacy by Arabs and missionaries, more than 50 percent of Ugandans can read and write—a high literacy rate compared with that of other African countries.

British officials in Buganda, who also appointed the chiefs.

In 1901 a railroad was established to provide fast transport to Uganda and to carry the new protectorate's agricultural produce through Kenya to the coast, and from there to ports all over the world. Cotton was introduced and soon became a major cash crop, as did coffee, which was native to Buganda, and tea. The British also built an excellent road system and a number of large boats for transport on Lake Victoria.

In 1939, Edward Frederick Mutesa II, thirty-third *kabaka* of Buganda, took the throne. Although the kingdom was still recognized by the British as an independent entity in Uganda, other ethnic groups outside Buganda were jostling for power. Milton Obote (oh BOH te) emerged as the leader of the northern-based Uganda Peoples' Congress. He

Along with cotton and coffee, tea is a cash crop in Uganda. Pickers harvest the tea leaves. ▼

formed an alliance with Mutesa II's royalist party, *Kabaka Yekka* (King Alone). Obote became prime minister, while Kabaka Mutesa II was installed as president. Their joint government took Uganda to independence, which was granted on October 9, 1962. Four years later, Obote declared himself executive president, and his troops, led by Colonel Idi Amin Dada, attacked the king's palace. Mutesa II—last king of Buganda—managed to escape to London, where he died in 1969, an exile. In 1967, Obote rewrote the country's constitution, made Uganda a republic, and abolished all the kingdoms.

In 1971, Idi Amin, calling himself Field Marshal "President for Life," overthrew Obote in a military coup. For the next 8 years, Amin's regime systematically plundered and destroyed Uganda—one of Africa's most thriving agriculturally-based communities. He also forced 50,000 Asians who had settled there to leave.

Kabaka Edward Frederick Mutesa II, last king of Buganda ▶

Today, Uganda still suffers from the British attempt to force "unity" on its different and competing ethnic groups. How would the region have fared if the British had not interfered? It is impossible to say for certain, but Buganda might at least have entered the twentieth century on its own terms.

Along the coast, on the other hand, colonial rule does not seem to have had such a dramatic impact—perhaps because the British concentrated their efforts on the inland regions of Kenya and Tanzania. There are signs of both continuity and change on the coast. Few dhows sail the Indian Ocean, and gold, slaves, and ivory are no longer market items. But the scent of cloves still clings to Zanzibar's streets, and the Suaheli women of Paté and Lamu go about their daily business much as they have always done. Now, however, the Europeans and other foreigners who throng what was once the ancient land of Zenj, clambering about the ruined palaces and mosques where great sultans once ruled, are tourists who have come for pleasure, not profit.

The shores of what was once the land of Zenj are now a tropical haven for tourists. ▶

Pronunciation Key

Some words in this book may be new to you or difficult to pronounce. Those words have been spelled phonetically in parentheses. The syllable that receives stress in a word is shown in small capital letters. The following pronunciation key shows how letters are used to show different sounds.

a	after	(AF tur)	oh	flow	(floh)	ch	chicken	(CHIHK un)
ah	father	(FAH thur)	oi	boy	(boi)	g	game	(gaym)
ai	care	(kair)	oo	rule	(rool)	ing	coming	(KUM ing)
aw	dog	(dawg)	or	horse	(hors)	j	job	(jahb)
ay	paper	(PAY pur)				k	came	(kaym)
			ou	cow	(kou)	ng	long	(lawng)
e	letter	(LET ur)	yoo	few	(fyoo)	s	city	(SIH tee)
ee	eat	(eet)	u	taken	(TAY kun)	sh	ship	(shihp)
				matter	(MAT ur)	th	thin	(thihn)
ih	trip	(trihp)	uh	ago	(uh goh)	thh	feather	(FETHH ur)
eye	idea	(eye DEE uh)				y	yard	(yahrd)
y	hide	(hyd)				z	size	(syz)
ye	lie	(lye)				zh	division	(duh VIHZH un)

For Further Reading
(* = Recommended for young readers)

Boyd, Herb. *African History for Beginners.* New York: Writers and Readers Publishing, 1991.*

Brooks, Lester. *Great Civilizations of Ancient Africa.* New York: Four Winds Press, 1971.*

Burton, Richard F. *The Lake Regions of Central Africa.* London: Longman, 1860.

Davidson, Basil. *Africa in History.* New York: Macmillan, 1991.

Davidson, Basil. *African Kingdoms.* New York: Time-Life Books, 1966.

Davidson, Basil. *A Guide to African History.* New York: Doubleday, Zenith Books, 1965.

Davidson, Basil. *The Lost Cities of Africa.* Boston: Little, Brown, 1970.

Dobler, Lavinia G. *Great Rulers of the African Past.* New York: Doubleday, 1965.*

Freeman-Grenville, G. S. P. *The East African Coast.* Oxford: Clarendon Press, 1962.

Joseph, Joan. *Black African Empires.* Franklin Watts, 1974.*

Harris, Joseph E. *Africans and Their History*. New York: New American Library, 1987.

Hugon, Anne. *The Exploration of Africa from Cairo to the Cape*. New York: Harry N. Abrams, 1993.*

Karugire, S. R. *A Political History of Uganda*. London: Heinemann Educational Books, 1980.

Kirkman, James S. *Men and Monuments of the East African Coast*. New York: Frederick Praeger, 1964.

Kiwanuka, S. *A History of Buganda*. New York: Africana Publishing, 1972.

Ki-Zerbo, Joseph. *Die Geschichte Schwarz-Afrikas* (The History of Black Africa). Wuppertal: Peter Hammer, 1979.

Knappert, J. *East Africa: Kenya, Tanzania, and Uganda*. New Delhi: Vikas, 1987.

Kwamena-Poh, Michael. *African History in Maps*. London: Longman, 1982.

Mazrui, Ali. *The Africans—A Triple Heritage*. Boston: Little, Brown, 1986.

McEvedy, Collin. *The Penguin Atlas of African History*. London: Penguin Books, 1980.*

Mukherjee, R. *Uganda: An Historical Accident?* Trenton: Africa World Press, 1985.

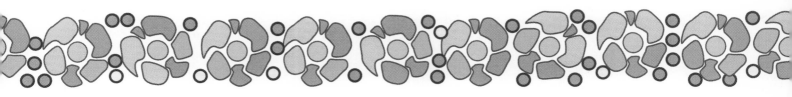

Murray, Jocelyn. *Cultural Atlas of Africa*. New York: Facts on File, 1989.*

Oliver, Roland. *The African Experience*. New York: HarperCollins, 1991.

Oliver, Roland, and J. D. Fage. *A Short History of Africa*. 6th ed. London: Penguin Books, 1988.

Perl, L. *History of East Africa*. New York: William Morrow, 1973.

Ray, Benjamin C. *Myth, Ritual and Kingship in Buganda*. New York: Oxford University Press, 1991.

Reusche, R. *History of East Africa*. New York: Fredrick Ungar, 1961.

Roscoe, John. *The Baganda*. London: Frank Cass, 1965.

Roscoe, John. *Twenty-Five Years in East Africa*. Cambridge: Cambridge University Press, 1921.

Speke, John Hanning. *Journal of the Discovery of the Source of the Nile*. London: N.P., 1863.

Stacey, Tom. *Peoples of the Earth*. Tom Stacey and Europa Verlag, 1972.*

Stanley, Henry M. *Through the Dark Continent*. New York: Harper & Brothers, 1878.

Thompson, Elizabeth Bartlett. *Africa Past and Present*. Boston: Houghton Mifflin, 1966.

Index

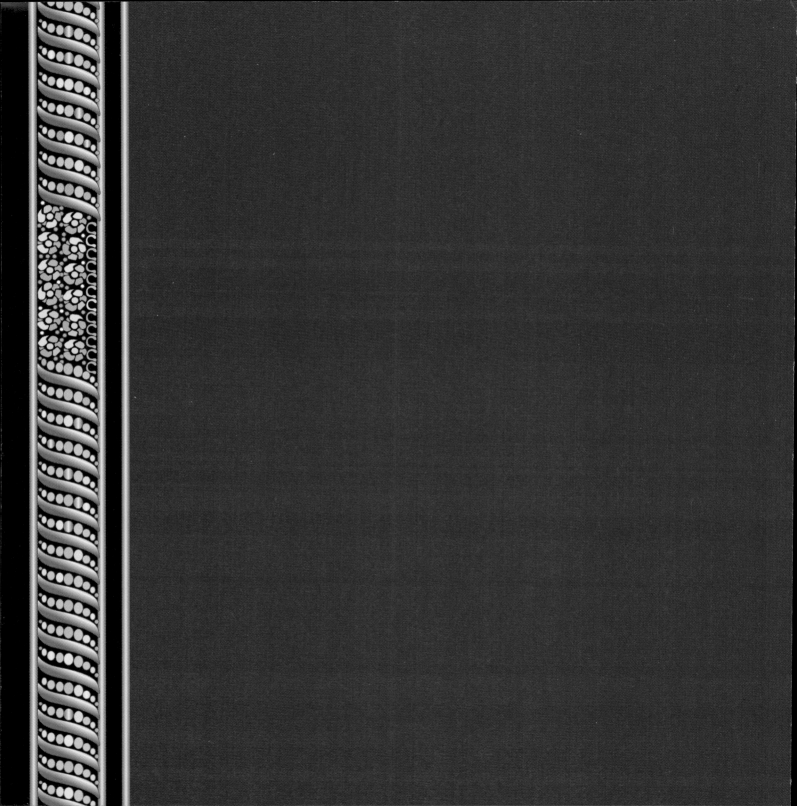